374

Understanding Staff Development

SRHE and Open University Press Imprint
General Editor: Heather Eggins

Current titles include:

Michael Abramson *et al.*: *Further and Higher Education Partnerships.*
Ronald Barnett: *Improving Higher Education*
Ronald Barnett: *Learning to Effect*
Ronald Barnett: *Limits of Competence*
Ronald Barnett: *The Idea of Higher Education*
Tony Becher: *Governments and Professional Education*
Robert Bell and Malcolm Tight: *Open Universities: A British Tradition?*
Hazel Bines and David Watson: *Developing Professional Education*
Jean Bocock and David Watson: *Managing the Curriculum*
David Boud *et al.*: *Using Experience for Learning*
Angela Brew: *Directions in Staff Development*
John Earwaker: *Helping and Supporting Students*
Roger Ellis: *Quality Assurance for University Teaching*
Gavin J. Fairbairn and Christopher Winch: *Reading, Writing and Reasoning: A Guide for Students*
Maureen Farish *et al.*: *Equal Opportunities in Colleges and Universities*
Shirley Fisher: *Stress in Academic Life*
Diana Green: *What is Quality in Higher Education?*
Sinclair Goodlad: *The Quest for Quality*
Susanne Haselgrove: *The Student Experience*
Jill Johnes and Jim Taylor: *Performance Indicators in Higher Education*
Ian McNay: *Visions of Post-compulsory Education*
Robin Middlehurst: *Leading Academics*
Henry Miller: *The Management of Change in Universities*
Jennifer Nias: *The Human Nature of Learning: Selections from the Work of M.L.J. Abercrombie*
Keith Noble: *Changing Doctoral Degrees*
Gillian Pascall and Roger Cox: *Women Returning to Higher Education*
Graham Peeke: *Mission and Change*
Moira Peelo: *Helping Students with Study Problems*
Kjell Raaheim *et al.*: *Helping Students to Learn*
Tom Schuller: *The Changing University*
Tom Schuller: *The Future of Higher Education*
Peter Scott: *The Meanings of Mass Higher Education*
Michael Shattock: *The UGC and the Management of British Universities*
John Smyth: *Academic Work*
Geoffrey Squires: *First Degree*
Ted Tapper and Brian Salter: *Oxford, Cambridge and the Changing Idea of the University*
Kim Thomas: *Gender and Subject in Higher Education*
Malcolm Tight: *Higher Education: A Part-time Perspective*
David Warner and Elaine Crosthwaite: *Human Resource Management in Higher and Further Education*
David Warner and Gordon Kelly: *Managing Educational Property*
David Warner and Charles Leonard: *The Income Generation Handbook*
Graham Webb: *Understanding Staff Development*
Sue Wheeler and Jan Birtle: *A Handbook for Personal Tutors*
Thomas G. Whiston and Roger L. Geiger: *Research and Higher Education*
Gareth Williams: *Changing Patterns of Finance in Higher Education*
John Wyatt: *Commitment to Higher Education*

Understanding Staff Development

Graham Webb

Society for Research into Higher Education
& Open University Press

Published by SRHE and
Open University Press
Celtic Court
22 Ballmoor
Buckingham
MK18 1XW

and 1900 Frost Road, Suite 101
Bristol, PA 19007, USA

First published 1996

A catalogue record of this book is available from the British Library

ISBN   0 335 19289 0 (hb)   0 335 19288 2 (pb)

Library of Congress Cataloging-in-Publication Data
Webb, Graham, 1950–
    Understanding staff development / Graham Webb.
        p.   cm.
    Includes bibliographical references and index.
    ISBN 0–335–19289–0. — ISBN 0–335–19288–2 (pbk.)
    1. College teaching.   2. College teachers—Training of.
    I. Title.
LB2331.W35   1996
378.1′25—dc20   95–33300
                                                                      CIP

Typeset by Graphicraft Typesetters Limited, Hong Kong
Printed in Great Britain by St Edmundsbury Press, Bury St Edmunds, Suffolk

Dedicated to Susan,
with love

Contents

Preface   ix

1   Introduction   1

2   Positive Knowledge and Progress in Staff Development   9

3   Staff Development for Understanding People and Ourselves   35

4   To Critically Go: Staff Development for a Better World   59

5   Postmodernity and Staff Development: Nowhere to Run   79

6   By Diverse Paths: Developing Staff Developers   99

References   113

Index   121

Preface

I started to write this book in November 1992. A couple of more 'practical' projects then intervened, followed by the recent flurry of activity occasioned by quality audit. The book has therefore been fairly long in gestation and delivery.

During this period I have been surprised that little in the way of similar or complementary material seems to have come from the educational and staff development discourse. For example, in this book I am critical of the idea of development which we receive from the past. I offer critiques of both action research and phenomenography (deep and surface approaches to learning). I suggest the fundamental significance of hermeneutics (interpretation) for staff development and see 'reflective practice' as a branch of the hermeneutical tree. I use the insights afforded by postmodernism. I am guarded on the issue of professionalism for staff development and, while seeing potential benefits, I am concerned about the risk of 'capture' (and thus conformity and orthodoxy) by those holding a particular view.

In short, I see staff development as a site for contestation. I hope that this book will provoke and stimulate the contest of ideas. I also hope that this will take place in the hermeneutical spirit of 'understanding' and 'love'. If you, the reader, have any comment which you would like to make to me directly, I would be delighted to hear from you.

Once again I acknowledge my thanks for the friendship and support of all those who make up the *whanau* of the Higher Education Research and Development Society of Australasia (HERDSA), and to Alan and Lauren for lighting my way.

Dr Graham Webb
Director, Higher Education Development Centre
University of Otago
PO Box 56, Dunedin, New Zealand

Phone: +64–3–479–8439
Fax: +64–3–479–8362
e-mail: GWebb@Gandalf.Otago.ac.nz

1

Introduction

The trouble is that the phrase 'staff development' is so all embracing that to say one favours and practises it has little more meaning than to say that one favours virtue and opposes sin – it could be anything and everything.

(A respondent quoted in Greenaway and Harding 1978: 12)

This book is about staff development. There are many definitions of staff development, but there is also a reasonable degree of convergence. Staff development is normally considered to include the institutional policies, programmes and procedures which facilitate and support staff so that they may fully serve their own and their institution's needs. Despite differences in their origins (and perhaps their destinations), 'staff development' and 'professional development' are currently read as one. In tertiary institutions such as universities, staff and/or professional development has mostly been concerned with educational development – the development of teaching and learning. Centres and units have grown up in most tertiary institutions to promote this development. Their titles are various but often contain words such as educational, academic, professional, research, advisory, teaching and learning.

This book maintains the traditional focus of educational development as a primary area for staff development. In so doing, it ignores some recent trends. Many development units are presently taking on wider roles concerning the professional development of staff with regard to research, management and a range of generic or human resource areas. Many are also merging with the institutional staff development provision for non-academic staff in order to provide staff development across the board. However, educational (teaching and learning) development is still a major concern of development units and their staff; it is the one upon which this book will concentrate.

Educational and staff development

I am an educational and staff developer working in higher education. Prior to this I was a 'normal' academic, teaching courses, publishing research, counselling students, taking on administrative tasks, and so on. My life nowadays is not entirely different, but neither is it the same. Like most educational and staff developers, I organize workshops, seminars and symposia on various topics, conduct teaching consultations with individual teachers or with course teams (I watch people teach) and carry out research and evaluation projects for my institution concerning academic and related matters. Educational and staff developers (such as I) tend to teach student courses in order to 'maintain our credibility' and increasingly we offer certificate, diploma or master's courses in tertiary teaching. Also increasingly, we participate in the 'quality' and 'audit' concerns of our institutions.

We can have an impact at many levels. We may consult with individual staff members having serious problems with their teaching. As we help them to improve their teaching, we might have a profound impact upon their academic careers, their confidence and well-being generally, and even their personal lives. We may assist in the provision of a well-designed and integrated system of initial workshops, mentoring and subsequent certification which ensures that new staff members are properly inducted into their work as teachers and researchers. Whether it be at the individual or institutional level, there is little doubt that educational and staff development now has a greater opportunity to make an impact and to be taken seriously than ever before. In a relatively short time, we have moved from cottage industry to institutional necessity.

Over the last 20 years, staff developers and others have been commenting about the place of development in higher education: the changes they believe should occur, as well as those that have occurred.[1] Recently, Warren Piper (1994) has attempted to trace the future of staff development units. He argues that in the past they have tended to be concerned almost totally with teaching and learning improvement, usually at the level of the individual academic. This is what he calls 'Model A', and it is predominantly an 'educational', 'teaching' or 'academic' development role. He sees this changing to 'Model B' as institutions become more conscious of the need to support organizational change and policy development. 'Model B' units will thus become more management- and policy-orientated and will serve a 'staff' rather than a narrowly 'educational' development role.

Throughout this book I will use the terms 'educational' and 'staff' development in conjunction, despite their somewhat different interpretations. Educational development is a subset of staff development, for, as we have already seen, staff development can include areas such as research, administration, management, community service and policy formation. Very many of the concerns and approaches raised in this book spring from educational issues, but have wider implications. There are also implications for staff development and training in settings other than higher education.

There are many ramifications for staff developers to consider if we are to follow the policy and management role realignment which Warren Piper predicts. However, it does not mean that there is an unbridgeable chasm between what we have been doing and what we will be doing. Nor does it mean that the institutional policy role will last for ever.

Boud and McDonald (1981) suggested three models which 'educational consultants' (i.e. developers) might adopt.[2] These were: professional service, counselling and colleagual. The professional service model casts the consultant as a provider of specialized services such as audio-visual aids, computer-assisted learning or multimedia. This being the case, it tends to marginalize the consultant as 'specialist expert' with a purely 'technical' orientation.

The counselling model sees the consultant as providing conditions 'under which academics can explore the nature of their teaching problems, and . . . help teachers reach an understanding of how they might be able to deal with problems which they have identified' (Boud and McDonald 1981: 5). The consultant provides a safe place for teachers (or students in student counselling centres) to discuss their problems and look for solutions. The main problem is in people being deterred from using a service which they see as being 'remedial'.

The colleagual model operates when developers and teachers collaborate on a joint research project to improve practice (e.g. an action research project). The strength of the approach is that it approximates activities with which academics are familiar, and the main weaknesses are that it lacks a service orientation and tends towards 'reinventing the wheel'. So Boud and McDonald (1981: 5) suggest that the best approach for educational and staff development is 'an eclectic approach' because 'in practice the educational consultant needs to draw from each of these models'. In a perceptive passage, they provide an outline which remains relevant today:

> It is necessary to work flexibly and eclectically in order to respond to the unique demands of each situation. The skills which need to be developed are those of each of the practitioners we have described: both technical competence and interpersonal skill are necessary, and the consultant's presentation to the rest of the educational community needs to be that of a colleague and fellow academic. At particular times and for particular teachers the consultant may need to adopt one or other of these roles exclusively, but if one approach takes over completely then effective development is likely to be hampered.

The three dimensions which Boud and McDonald identify find corollaries in various chapters of this book, in particular the areas of positive knowledge for technical expertise; human understanding; and collaboration for practical and social improvement. The eclectic approach advocated by Boud and McDonald also finds voice in the partial and fractured nature of our work as it is interpreted in the postmodern condition. In all of this, educational and staff development can be seen to reflect broader areas in the theory of knowledge and the world of ideas.

Where Warren Piper sees a clear movement from Model A to Model B, Boud and McDonald's 'eclectic' blending of the dimensions of staff development allows for greater continuity. Moving towards an institutional, policy-linked role does not necessarily take us out of our more customary practices; rather, it changes the landscape. For example, in Chapters 3 and 6 of this book I will consider the human face of understanding, empathy, Being and various kinds of staff development relationships. Developers may be comfortable with much of this in the context of working with a teacher to improve their teaching, but uncomfortable in the context of working with senior managers in the development of policy initiatives. But in this new situation the understanding and experience of the staff developer may be no less important. For example, in working with senior managers a developer may well be talking to a different set of human beings, but human beings they remain. The skills the developer may have acquired in terms of facilitation, communication, human understanding, empathy and the ability to act as confidant or counsellor, may be appreciated none the less in the different context.

In short, although I believe staff development is changing, and changing in a direction similar to that outlined by Warren Piper, this does not mean that we should feel overly disorientated or threatened. Some of the ways in which we are already prepared for the change have to do with our experience of human understanding and empathy, others concern our orientation towards human dignity and social justice, and still others concern our abilities in criticism of the status quo and the indeterminacy of modern development practice. Each of these areas contributes to our understanding of teaching and learning development, as outlined in the following chapters. In short, there are ways in which we operate at present which will help us to prepare for change in the various orientations, positions, demands, roles and directions which will confront us in the future.

Staff developer/teacher . . . teacher/student

Throughout this book I will be talking about education and learning. An immediate consequence is the need to refer to 'teacher' and 'student'. I make an underlying assumption that the educative relationship between teacher and student is reflected in the educative relationship between staff developer and teacher. Much has been written on metaphors which people use to encapsulate their ideas about teaching and learning, and the relationship between teacher and student (e.g. Fox 1983; Kloss 1987). There is also much to be learned from the teacher education literature with regard to teachers' stories and the ways in which their views concerning education come into being and change over time (e.g. Letiche 1990; Elbaz 1991;

Calderhead and Robson 1991). Many of the differing metaphors which encapsulate the teaching of students find their corollaries in staff developers' views of their task.

But there are also some important differences. The normal relationship between teacher and student is partly defined by an acknowledged 'academic' difference between the two. The teacher is assumed to be at a higher level and to know more about both the subject and the teaching of the subject. Attempts to effect more participatory or emancipatory teaching bear witness to this. However, the relationship between developer and teacher is somewhat different as, for the most part, both have academic status.

Staff developers usually move into the area after experience as a subject teacher. Because of this experience it is likely that they will have an academic status advantage over the younger members of staff with whom they are working. This tends to make the relationship somewhat nearer to that of teacher–student. In other cases, however, the developer may be consulted by a person with higher academic status or greater experience and thus have to establish credibility (earn respect) by his/her actions, rather than assume the respect granted by position. This mirrors the situation of the teacher confronted with mature students or students with work experience in that such teachers need to establish a credibility which is somewhat beyond the norm.

The developer may have formal qualifications in a number of domains such as the subject area (master's or PhD), education (postgraduate certificate, diploma or master's degree in higher education), and, perhaps increasingly in the future, a qualification as an educational and staff developer. The developer may also establish or maintain credibility as a teacher by continuing to teach (student) courses; as a supervisor, by continuing to supervise research students; as a researcher, by continuing to publish; as an administrator by heading a unit or part of a unit; as an institutional policy adviser, by demonstrating clear vision, organizational planning and review at the unit or other levels.

But it is the relationship that developers form with their 'clients' which is crucial. For the most part a teacher's relationship with a student may last a semester or a year. Sometimes it lasts over three years and occasionally (as with a research student) longer than this. For a developer, the relationship with a 'client' is often a long-term proposition. The relationship between developer and teacher remains after a particular project or encounter, albeit in dormant form. On the other hand, the developer–teacher relationship is unlikely to be as close or frequent as the relationship between teaching colleagues within a department. The developer–teacher relationship is thus likely to be different from both teacher–student and teacher–teacher relationships. This having been said, a theme of this book is that there is still much that can be learned from the general educational (teacher–student, teaching–learning) literature which has implications for educational and staff development practice.

About this book

This book asks what educational and staff development might mean when we view the world and ourselves in certain ways. In the chapters which follow, different ways of viewing the world and our place in it will be outlined, with each view acting as a context for interpreting the task of the educational and staff developer.

As a staff developer, I know how difficult it is to find time to consider ideas from a broad range of knowledge and to think about the implications of ideas for my busy, daily practice. Writing this book has forced me to do just this, and as a result has changed my conception of the role I play as an educational and staff developer. In particular, it has challenged me to accept discontinuity in the role. At one time I would have been tempted to explain what I do and how and why I do it, in terms of a coherent theory or model. A recent book in the area attempts exactly this:

> Professional development in higher education has often been criticised for lacking a sound theoretical framework. The present book is an attempt to fill this gap by building a theoretical model that integrates theory and practice, educational research and teaching in higher education.
>
> (Zuber-Skerritt 1992: 1)

I am no longer sure that this is desirable. Writing this book has caused me to confront the *various* sources from which I attempt to legitimate what I do. It has also caused me to take a little further some critical thoughts concerning the theories and practices which are popular with people working in the area.

Apart from educational and staff developers within higher education, what I have to say may be of interest to educators generally, as well as to staff developers and trainers outside education. The scope of the book is more general than specific. And while I hope that the book will have an effect upon the practice of development or training, it is certainly not intended to be a 'practical' book. This makes it a little odd, as educational and staff development tends to lead relentlessly toward the practical. I have written elsewhere that:

> [f]or development to be seen as worthwhile, for it to establish credibility in terms of the 'market' (the 'practitioners' for whom it is intended), development has needed to prove its essential and immediate practicality. The practical has been valued over (and often defined in opposition

to) the theoretical, and especially the philosophical. In short, practitioners tend to want answers, rather than further questions.

(Webb 1992a: 352)

So do developers. Our conferences and workshops are lively and boisterous bazaars in which we are urged to try out new activities and new techniques with our students or clients. Our most popular books suggest '53 interesting things' for ourselves and our clients to try. We demand new activities to stimulate teaching, learning or other staff development concerns, and recently there has been no shortage of vendors.

There is a formal literature, too, which gives a basis for some of these activities. That literature suggests why we should be attempting to develop teaching and learning in certain directions. It gives various conceptions of 'the good' in teaching, learning and educational development. For example, some of the most pervasive themes currently are of reflective practice, 'deep' and 'surface' approaches to learning, and emancipatory action research.

Both the practical activities and the research literature (which support each other) cause me some concern. I believe they offer only a limited spectrum of the orientations to knowledge and practice which we might adopt. I know that they exclude some of my own experience: the rich experience of human Being which I know is important in my work. However, if I try to justify what I do and the way I do it, I find myself ill-prepared. So, while I have some sympathy with the ideas of reflective practice, 'deep' and 'surface' approaches to learning and action research, I have some concerns, too. I have found it difficult to articulate my concerns and to find critiques in the literature which can help me.

This book represents my attempt to explain such concerns and to point to areas that have not attracted much attention from staff developers, but which I think are important. Such areas include consideration of the whole notion of 'development' and 'progress'; the tradition of 'human science', interpretation, empathy and the importance of Being; and the areas of postmodernism, post-structuralism and deconstruction. As the book unfolds, I attempt to sketch some of the implications of the ideas which lie within these areas.

Finally

Staff and educational development as it is now conceived is a relatively recent phenomenon. Over the past 20 years or so it has striven to find a place, a rationale, a secure anchoring point for the prescriptions and practices it produces. In the next chapters a number of possible anchoring points will be discussed.

Rorty (1979) has warned against 'systematic' philosophy and its attempts to provide us with secure foundations. He prefers to speak of philosophy as 'edifying'. By this he means that the conversation of philosophy should be an open-ended and enlightening one, rather than one possessed by the search for closure and foundational explanation. Foundational anchoring points for educational and staff development are equally illusive. However, my hope is that readers will find the quest both as interesting and as enlightening as it has been for the writer.

Notes

1. See, for example, SDU/UTMU Institute of Education (1975); Elton and Simmonds (1976); Greenaway and Harding (1978); Teather (1979); Rhodes and Hounsell (1980); Harding *et al.* (1981); Matheson (1981); Bligh (1982); Cannon (1983); Mathias and Rutherford (1985); Main (1985); Smith (1992).
2. For other metaphors and models of educational staff development see Harding *et al.* (1981) and Zuber-Skerritt (1992).

2

Positive Knowledge and Progress in Staff Development

... specialists without spirit, sensualists without heart, caught in the delusion that they have achieved a level of development never before attained by mankind.

(Weber 1948: 182)

Introduction

Staff developers are frequently called upon to answer questions regarding teaching and learning. For example, is lecturing an effective way of teaching; what is the optimum size for a tutorial group; are multiple-choice tests a better form of assessment than essays; can teaching performance be measured?

How do we, as educational and staff developers, answer such questions? Apart from being developers, we are teachers, too, and as such may have opinions based upon our own experience. We may also have intuitions of what we consider to be 'good' or 'valuable' in teaching. We might consider the questions to be unanswerable, or at least unanswerable without clarification or definition of some of the words used in the questions. But given clarification, is it possible that there *could* be answers to questions such as these, and could we regard such answers as establishing a truth over and above our own experience and proclivity? When colleagues ask us such questions, it is often in the belief that there are clear and unambiguous answers which we, as 'experts' or 'specialists', must know. There must be a research literature in which the answers can be found. Somewhere, there must be 'positive' knowledge: objective, proven, verified and accepted.

It is the attempt to construct such knowledge which is the central concern of this chapter. For developers and teachers the question is 'how can we judge differing approaches (to teaching, for example) one with another?' A standard is needed by which options can be evaluated, a 'gold standard' for knowledge, as it were. Should such a foundational and objective standard be produced, then it would be possible for us to judge one teaching method against another, one view of professional practice against another, and to chart an uncontroversial path of development based upon this 'certain' or 'positive' knowledge. Staff development in each of its areas of concern could then be viewed as a science for the improvement of its clients according to a recognized standard of knowledge. The basis for a programme such as this is found in a view of the world according to the philosophy of 'positive' knowledge, or positivism.

This chapter will consider the major elements of positivism and will offer a critique of the positivist position based upon an historical and a social interpretation of science. It will range further than that, however, in trying to illuminate the historical background to positivism and the Enlightenment era, an era in which the very ideas of progress and development were so implicitly bound. This will lead into the area of evolutionary theory and the biological metaphors that have fashioned our understanding of development, which in turn will lead to the birth of modern psychology, its early influences and some of the problems associated with its world-view. Some of the implications of this wide-ranging discussion for educational and staff development will then be discussed.

Background to positive knowledge and positivism

> The term *truth* usually precipitates one of two sets of associations. The first, as found in most traditional forms of metaphysics and theology, defines truth in terms of the absolute, the complete, and the changeless. The other, represented by much of modern science and by analytical forms of philosophy, defines truth in terms of what is logically or empirically verifiable.
>
> (DiCenso 1990: xiii)

Positivism is a view of the world which seeks to base knowledge on rational, logical and empirically verifiable information. It is knowledge in which we can be positive: it is positive knowledge. If such knowledge is obtainable, then it can form the anchoring point in our search for truth. It means we can abandon our earlier attachments to truth via metaphysics and theology, in favour of scientifically established knowledge. While this possibility may seem commonplace today, it should be remembered that in the history of Western philosophy, metaphysical and theological accounts of truth for long held sway.

In the fifth century BC, for example, Plato articulated a view of knowledge which has exerted a profound influence ever since. In sketch form, Plato's view was that the world as we know it is comprised of transitory, changeable and often deceptive events. We must therefore be careful to distinguish the naïve impressions of the world which we obtain through the *senses* from essential truths which may only be procured by contemplation through the *mind*. This is an 'idealist' position as opposed to a 'realist' one. An idealist sees truth as transcending the everyday world of sensory experience, whereas a realist sees truth as residing in that world – in reality. For Plato, every object or event in the 'real world' is an imperfect example of an ideal form. While we might draw thousands of circles, for example, each is an imperfect and evanescent representation of the perfect, essential form 'circle', which we can only appreciate in contemplation.

Applying this to teaching, the sensory, real-world experience we have of a form such as 'the lecture' should not obscure the ideal or perfect form which can only be approached through thoughtful imagination. Similar applications might be found in our stumbling attempts to introduce mere shadows of the ideals implied by 'student autonomy', 'student-directed learning', 'a deep approach to learning', 'teachers as reflective practitioners', 'collegiality' and so on. For the idealist the essence of knowledge and truth is to be achieved by thought and contemplation: the mind is the vehicle for taking us outside our immediate reality to the principles and transcendent truths which lie beyond.

Plato's ideal forms provided a world-view of order and stability which was appropriated in the Middle Ages of the Western world under the metaphysics of the Catholic Church. The Christian notion of God became the transcendent form; it provided the origin and substance for explanation and understanding of the world and humanity. While the nature of truth and knowledge was a matter for theological explanation, the economic and political system of feudalism also grounded the everyday experience of people in confirmed social roles, stability and permanence.

This sense of permanence was challenged around the year 1500 by the 'discovery' of the 'New World', the Renaissance and the Reformation, the three monumental events which mark the cessation of the Middle Ages and the beginning of modern times (Habermas 1987a). By the late eighteenth and early nineteenth centuries, and closely connected with the French Revolution, the *Zeitgeist* (spirit of the age: *Zeitgeist* itself being a new word of and for the time) was of a new age, a modern age, an era of Enlightenment.

The Enlightenment was inspired by advances in science and later technology, to the point where it seemed to some that entry to the essential truths of the universe was imminent. A slightly less extreme view described the spirit of the age as the infinite progress of scientific knowledge, and as the infinite advance towards social and moral betterment. In other words, human beings need no longer be constrained by the metaphysical systems which had hitherto bound them, as there are rational and logical laws which can be discovered to explain not only the natural world, but also social, economic and political institutions.

The foundation for the discovery of these laws was the rational human being: the final anchoring point for this view of the world. Descartes's famous *'cogito ergo sum'* ('I think therefore I am') encapsulates this notion of each person as a separate, conscious being. Our thinking is what makes us human and gives us 'being'. Kant completed the picture by characterizing thinking as reasoning and thus installed reason as the supreme arbiter available to the self-conscious, reflective and critical individual.

As the unified view of the world from the standpoint of religion and metaphysics fell apart, old problems concerned with truth, normative rightness (how one should act) and beauty assumed a different guise. Max Weber described how truth was coming to be adjudicated as a matter of knowledge according to science; justice and morality as the province of jurisprudence, moral theory and civil law; and beauty as the domain of institutionalized art criticism. Each domain comes under the control of specialists, expert in the application of rational and logical reasoning, so that each may develop according to its own inner logic. In short, Enlightenment thinkers (epitomized by Condorcet) expected that science and the arts would lead to the control of natural forces, the justice of social institutions, moral progress, an understanding of self and the happiness of human beings.

Positivism

Use of the word 'positivism' is linked with a number of French writers of the nineteenth century, and especially with Auguste Comte. As part of the new, modern age, and in accord with Enlightenment ideals, positivism was founded in the belief that 'positive' evidence (meaning 'scientific' or 'certain') was the only valid evidence for the advancement of knowledge. Positivism ruled out 'intangible' knowledge such as the metaphysical, theological and non-empirical. All 'non-sensory' knowledge claims were of this intangible nature, they could be dismissed as 'nonsense' and confined to the realm of irrationality, value judgement or belief. This was seen as a major advance in the liberation of knowledge from entrenched religious dogma and transcendental justification.

Comte himself was a trained mathematician who held mathematical logic to lie at the foundation of all science. The route to the mathematical and logical relationships of science lay in the observation of physical phenomena and induction from observations to the underlying laws. In similar vein, he saw observation as the foundation of social enquiry. By disciplined, objective observation and the application of mathematical logic, society would advance out of the earlier theological and metaphysical stages of development to the highest form of civilization, the positive or scientific, and this was a natural law of progress.

The high point of positivism was articulated by the 'Vienna Circle' of analytical philosophers and logical empiricists (or logical positivists) during the 1930s. By this time scientific method had been formalized away from the inductivist approach of Comte and the early French positivists in favour of the 'hypothetico-deductive' method. This saw all scientific enquiry proceeding by the advance of hypotheses deduced from general laws in order to explain unknowns or solve problems. A hypothesis could only be tested empirically and by recourse to observation and experiment. If the hypothesized occurrence (effect, reaction, etc.) was actually observed, then the hypothesis was confirmed, and this in turn supported the general law.

In this account, method is all. The method establishes objective truth in the sense of truth separate from all spatial and temporal vagaries. Truth is truth, separate from and standing above the society or time in which it is produced. Facts (empirical data) are facts; they are theory-free and unaffected by any spatially or temporally conditioned motives, prejudices or ideologies of the observer. Facts can be described in an observation language which does not have any theoretical prejudice or presupposition of its own. Hypotheses are verifiable only by empirical observation, and observational acts must be capable of replication by all (men) of good will following a similar process. Herein lie the principles of *verification* and of *replication* (which along with value freedom and theory independence of observation) are essential features of the positive account of knowledge.

Critiques of positivism

The positivist view holds the method of science to be the basis for any legitimate claim to knowledge, and rational action may *only* proceed on the basis of positive knowledge. As Berlin (1969: 43) notes, Comte's view of history and science was 'of one complete and all embracing pyramid of scientific knowledge; one method; one truth; one scale of rational, "scientific" values'. If no other form of knowledge is an acceptable basis for action, and if scientific knowledge and truth are synonymous, then it seems that we have indeed found the gold standard upon which to base our educational and staff development activities. However, the positive view of knowledge is more controversial than the account given so far allows, and the central tenets of the positivist account have attracted much critical attention.

One of the most influential critiques of positivist scientific method was launched by Karl Popper. Firstly, he considered the inductive account of knowledge formation which held that science could prove the truth of a general law by the taking of more and more empirical observations, each of which confirmed the law. Popper argued that no matter how many instances of confirming observations could be demonstrated, there was no way of discounting with certainty the possibility of an observation which would *not* confirm the law. A general law therefore could not be 'proved correct', 'proved true' or verified by inductive means. On the other hand, just one (recognized and agreed) observation which *falsified* the law would be enough to refute it. The point of science is thus *not* verification, but instead challenge and refutation of 'conjectures' advanced to explain a particular set of circumstances or events (Popper 1969).

This turning of the essential positivist position also highlighted a fundamental discrepancy in the account of truth through knowledge confirmation and verification. In short, if the only knowledge which is acceptable is that which can be empirically verified, where is the empirical knowledge which verifies the principle of verification (see, for example, Morris 1966)? Without this, according to the tenets of positivism, the principle of verification, a corner-stone of the positivist position, is no more than a metaphysical or *a priori* assumption, to be believed or not according to one's metaphysical inclination.

The second major contribution of Popper was with regard to the nature of empirical observation. He called into question the supposedly value-neutral observations of value-neutral observers, preferring instead an account of even the most basic observational statements as 'theory impregnated':

> observation is a process in which we play an intensely active part. We do not 'have' an observation (as we may 'have' a sense experience) but we 'make' an observation ... An observation is always preceded by ... something theoretical.
>
> (Popper 1972: 342)

Popper considers all people, scientists included, to be living at the centre of a 'horizon of expectations' which 'confers meaning or significance on our experiences, actions and observations' (Popper 1972: 345).

Popper may thus be seen as having a major influence on conceptions of what science is about, and what science can and cannot do. In the Popperian account, it is not possible to prove or verify scientific theories, only to challenge and possibly refute 'conjectures' which are advanced as explanations. Scientific knowledge is provisional, reason and rationality are essentially *critical* in nature rather than foundational: progress is achieved through critique and refutation rather than the assembly of truthful propositions upon secure foundations. The scientific investigator emerges from the shadows and is no longer seen as the value-free, passive and objective perceiver of 'facts', but instead as active in their constitution. The observations and observational language of the investigator are theory impregnated by the historical moment which influences the values and ideologies of the investigator through his or her 'horizon of expectations'. All of this leads away from the popular view of particular investigators 'discovering' 'objective truth' about 'reality', and towards the importance of shared understanding, intersubjective agreement and the role of a community of scientists:

what distinguishes scientific knowledge is not so much its logical status, as the fact that it is the outcome of a process of enquiry which is governed by critical norms and standards of rationality . . . scientific objectivity is not that which corresponds to some neutral reality. Rather, 'objective' reality is itself that which corresponds to the intersubjective agreement of a community of enquirers whose deliberations are conducted in accordance with shared standards of rationality.

(Carr and Kemmis 1986: 121–2)

Popper, however, did not follow his insights through to what might be considered their ultimate conclusion. He advanced a 'correspondence theory of truth' in which objective facts (reality), separate from the subjective, language-based accounts of the conscious and knowing investigator, came together in a 'third world' of theories, problems and arguments. In this way he was able to hold on to the notion of a separate reality, independent of the observer and agreed, formal procedures of observation and method. It is here that the Popperian view runs into difficulty, for if observations are always theory impregnated then it is impossible to make the single 'true' or value-free observation which he sees as necessary to refute a conjecture.

this means that theories can never be conclusively falsified because observation statements can never be theory-neutral and can never be conclusively true. In short, Popper's account requires that observation statements remain independent of theories, while at the same time conceding that this is not possible.

(Carr and Kemmis 1986: 120)

If observation statements are theory-laden, then the contest for a truthful account becomes a matter of argument between the holders of different theoretical positions and their respective interpretation (or constitution) of 'the facts', rather than the testing of theories against objective reality. It is here that the work of Thomas Kuhn has been highly influential.

Kuhn (1970) challenged the view of science as cumulative, both in the naïve positivist sense and in the Popperian sense of progression by refutation according to objective facts. Instead, he claims that scientific change occurs when a *paradigm* (a complex of assumptions, beliefs, language usage and observations) within which explanation has hitherto been based, comes under challenge. A paradigm originates when like-minded investigators form a community which can share common agreement about assumptions with regard to ontology (theory of what *is*, of being, *a priori* assumptions), epistemology (theory of knowledge) and methodology (how investigation may proceed). When there are alternative paradigms in competition with each other over explanation, their respective validities cannot be weighed according to 'objective reality' or 'the facts', as the differing paradigms present differing accounts of these, and objective observation outside of a theoretical (or paradigmatic) position is not possible. Thus, although:

> each may hope to convert the other to his way of seeing his science and its problems, neither may hope to prove his case. The competition between paradigms is not the sort of battle that can be resolved by proofs.
>
> (Kuhn 1970: 148)

Alternative paradigms are thus *incommensurable*, there being no 'meta-paradigm', as it were, from which to judge respective claims to validity, and no possibility of theory-free and objective factual data. The illusion of objectivity may arise when a paradigm remains unchallenged for some time, thus allowing widespread intersubjective sharing of beliefs, assumptions, language and the constitution of 'facts'. This is a time of 'normal science' when 'puzzles' may be solved within the paradigm without ever calling into question basal (paradigmatic) intersubjective agreement. It is only at a time of 'paradigm shift', when the normal assumptions and procedures fail to provide adequate answers, that the agreement which has previously been beyond dispute is called into question, and the possibility of viewing problems from an alternative paradigmatic stance may be raised. Progress in science has thus, on the face of it, more to do with the politics of power than with the revelation of ultimate truth. Progress in science can best be interpreted within social, political and historical contexts; it has lost its status as a vehicle for the progressive explanation of the ahistoric and asocial truths of reality.

If the importance of Kuhn's work may be judged by the intensity of the debate which followed its publication, then it was indeed epochal, resounding beyond the philosophy, history and sociology of science into social theory, art, literature, mythology, religion and elsewhere (Beyer 1988). Much effort was expended on trying to define exactly what Kuhn meant by the word 'paradigm', but perhaps the most sustained problem was seen as his inability to account for what was taken to be self-evident progress in the explanatory power of science. Kuhn himself made it clear that he, too, believes in underlying scientific values and attitudes and an evolutionary view of scientific progress which may be seen in terms of such things as greater accuracy and quantification of prediction, replacement of everyday by esoteric subject matter, the increasing number of different problems solved, simplicity, scope, and compatibility with other specialities:

> scientific development is, like biological, a unidirectional and irreversible process. Later scientific theories are better than earlier ones for solving puzzles ... That is not a relativist's position, and it displays the sense in which I am a convinced believer in scientific progress.
>
> (Kuhn 1970: 205–6)

Kuhn thus holds on to an essentially Enlightenment notion of science as a unidirectional and inexorable continuation of the progress of rationality. In this he appears to approach other writers who have argued against paradigm theory and for a 'coherentist' view of knowledge: a view which expresses faith in the 'coherence' of conditions for valid theory from differing standpoints (Evers 1991). So although Kuhn provides much ammunition to be used against Enlightenment tenets of progress and for, as we shall see later, post-structural accounts of change based on power, he did not follow this line himself. This stands in contrast to another notorious advocate of the 1960s movement towards a social interpretation of science, Paul Feyerabend.

By a historical examination of scientific method and how scientific changes actually come about, Feyerabend argues for human and socially grounded explanation including elements of 'irrationality'. For example, he claims that Galileo's case for confirming the Copernican hypothesis of the motion of the world (and thus a major revolution in physics), prevailed because of Galileo's 'style, and his clever techniques of persuasion, because he writes in Italian rather than in Latin, and because he appeals to people who are temperamentally opposed to the old ideas and the standards of learning connected with them'(Feyerabend 1975: 13). The only sensible principle for scientific method Feyerabend can detect is 'anything goes', and he produces a powerful argument 'against method' and in favour of an anarchistic theory of knowledge. His identification of rhetoric as a pervasive element in science, his argument for anarchism and against rationalism in the theory of knowledge, and his advocacy of the creativity of the scientist against the institutionalized authority and dogma of science, all foreshadow postmodern positions which are considered later in this book.

Evolution, progress and development

Thus far we have seen how the positive view of knowledge emerged from its historical origins in the Enlightenment, and how positivism may be viewed as an all-embracing attempt to ground objective knowledge in the methods of science. We have also seen some of the objections to this view and critiques of positivism which stress the social nature of scientific change. Before considering the implications of positivism for educational and staff development, it is necessary to sketch some further elements of the Enlightenment legacy, which have been influential in shaping the way in which we conceive of development. These concern the areas of biological evolution and the associated growth of modern psychology.

For the most part, traditional views of the world were static, with God forming the world, plants and mankind, just as they are today. Following Plato and Aristotle, and the later synthesis of Greek philosophy with medieval

Christianity, each species was seen as having a typical form (a reflection of an ideal form) which was maintained through reproduction from one generation to the next: 'The hierarchy of natural forms stretching from the most primitive up to man – the 'chain of being' – represented a complete and hence absolutely fixed plan of creation' (Bowler 1989: 5).

The idea of evolution challenged this fixed view of creation. In its earliest biological sense, evolution was used as a means of describing the growth of an embryo in the womb. At first it was thought that this was no more than the expansion of a preformed miniature of the complete organism (pre-formation theory), but by 1800 this had been abandoned in favour of a concept of construction from unformed matter towards a final product.

There is an important point to note here, in that *ontogeny* (the origins and development of the *individual*), in so far as it uses the growth of an embryo as a model, gives the impression that 'living structures ascend a fixed pattern of development toward a predetermined goal' (Bowler 1989: 9). This embryo metaphor – the idea of development as directed towards a given end and passing through a number of predetermined stages – has been elaborated in a number of theories of learning and teaching, and of cognitive and moral development. It will thus be helpful here to consider what it is we think we are talking about when we use the words development, progress and evolution. In terms of ontogeny (individuals), 'evolution' and 'development' appear to be used interchangeably, and selected definitions taken from the *Oxford English Dictionary* underline this convergence:

> *Development* . . . growth and unfolding of what is in the germ . . . evolu-tion or bringing out from a latent or elementary condition . . . bring-ing out of the latent capabilities of anything . . . gradual advancement through progressive stages . . . growth from within.

> *Evolution* . . . process of unrolling, opening out, or disengaging from an envelope . . . opening out or unfolding of what is wrapped up . . . appearance in orderly succession of a long train of events . . . develop-ing or working out in detail what is implicitly or potentially contained in an idea or principle . . . development of a design . . . development or growth according to its inherent tendencies . . . the rise or origi-nation of anything by natural development, as distinguished from its production by a specific act; 'growing' as opposed to 'being made'.

Both development and evolution have essentially ahistoric and asocial con-notations of change in a given direction over a given time towards a given end. 'Progress' adds to the cluster of meaning by bringing the idea of spatial change, movement in space of a given direction towards a given end.

Progress . . . stepping or marching forward or onward . . . journeying . . .
travelling . . . onward movement in space . . . move forward, advance
as opposed to rest or regress . . . going on to a further or higher stage
. . . growth, development, advance to better and better conditions
. . . improve . . . proceed, as the terms or items of a series, from less
to greater; to form an advancing series . . . to make regular progress
toward completion.

Evolution in the sense of *phylogeny* (development of *species* or natural
history) originally carried with it similar implications to those of ontogeny.
Herbert Spencer, who introduced and did most to popularize the term 'evolution' (it was seldom used by Darwin), portrayed it as a process of cosmic
progress and the inevitable development of life towards higher forms. However, both Spencer and Darwin broke with the embryo metaphor, in that
they conceived of progress as open-ended rather than directed toward a
single goal, such as man (Bowler 1989: 9). But Spencer rather than Darwin
typified the popular view of evolution which is still with us today, and which
conceives evolution as progress and advance towards higher levels of organization. We see here how the Enlightenment *Zeitgeist* of progress could
be interpreted within biology as theories of development and evolution.
Spencer himself appears to have used the terms evolution, development
and progress virtually interchangeably (Kessen 1990; Morss 1990). Spencer-
ian biological evolution was thus in step with Condorcet's historically inevitable human, social, scientific and technological progress, and similarly with
Comte's account of historical progress towards positivism.

The social implications of Darwin's view of evolution are complex. Bowler
(1989: 282–3) notes how:

liberalism and socialism were able to adapt the idea of natural selection to their own purposes. It is impossible to see social Darwinism as
a simple and obvious application of the Darwinian theory to man.
Links between biology and social thought could be established in many
different ways . . .

The usual account of social Darwinism has competition, the struggle for
existence and the elimination of the 'unfit' as the hallmarks of progress
viewed from the standpoint of Victorian capitalism. There is little doubt
that Darwin was influenced to some degree by Adam Smith's *Wealth of Nations*
(1776), in which it was argued that prosperity depended upon the freedom
of individuals to act on their own initiative, unfettered by any form of state
intervention. This was part of a wider utilitarian view in which the greatest
happiness could be ensured for the greatest number by allowing individual
autonomy and freedom. When translated into Smith's *laissez-faire* economics,
it could be seen as a *natural* process which ensured that individuals of ability and initiative would be rewarded. But as Bowler noted above, translation

of utilitarianism into Darwinism, Darwinian evolution into social theory, or indeed *any* biological theory into a programme for human and social action, is fraught with difficulty. Perhaps the best we can do is to pick out some of the main ideas from this area which could have implications for educational and staff development.

A first consideration is the equation of development with a view of ontogeny as revealed in the embryo metaphor. This carries with it expectations of the inevitable unfolding of sequential and natural stages towards a predetermined end. It stands in contrast to both modern experimental embryology and to Darwinian phylogeny, in both of which the open-endedness of the process is acknowledged. For example, with respect to phylogeny and evolution, Mivart's comments on Darwin still stand: 'it is clear and indisputable that the Darwinian hypothesis was one essentially opposed to the assertion of a purpose or design in nature' (quoted in Young 1985: 121).

But Darwin's 'purposeless' view of evolution is not the message that has been attached to conceptions of development. Instead, the 'embryo metaphor' of development has proven to be more durable, especially with regard to the theory of recapitulation. Recapitulation suggests not only that is individual (ontogenic) development determined, but also that developmental stages repeat or *recapitulate* earlier stages of species (phylogenic) evolution. Development in the human embryo, for example, recapitulates the earlier evolutionary history of human beings in full, gills and all (see Gould 1977). Although later discredited by Mendelian genetics, recapitulation has had a powerful influence on learning theory as well as criminal anthropology, racism, and Freudian and Jungian psychoanalysis (Gould 1977).

A final consideration is the view of humans as differentiated individuals who nevertheless *naturally* constitute a larger and single social entity. It is to do with the conflation of 'species' and 'society'.

> [An] attitude that went far deeper than any particular biological theory was the tendency to think of human differences in hierarchical terms. Eugenics and social Darwinism were based on a ranking of individuals within a single society. Some were assumed to be naturally abler than others, a fact reflected in the division of society into higher and lower classes.
>
> (Bowler 1989: 285)

The direction taken by this argument is towards the ranking of individuals in terms of their 'natural abilities': a direction which led towards the science of eugenics (assisting natural selection by selective human breeding), the associated ranking and evolutionary placement (superior–inferior) of races, and to the birth of modern psychology. With its links to evolutionary thought, its wholehearted embrace of positivism, and (as will be argued later in this chapter) its importance for educational and staff development, it is worth-while elaborating a few points concerning psychology and the ways in which it has been constituted.

Psychology

In the fifteenth century psychology was concerned with study of the soul and spiritual being, but it was later secularized towards the *philosophical* study of mental phenomena. The origins of modern psychology may once more be traced to the growth of faith in reason and science which epito-mized the Enlightenment. By the late nineteenth century this resulted in the creation of experimental laboratories and by the early twentieth century there was a remarkably consistent view of psychology (shared by leading figures such as Galton, Pearson, James, Cattell, Watson, Hall, Thorndike and Terman) as scientific rather than philosophical (Olssen 1991). This scientific self-view was also thoroughly positivist.

A major repercussion of psychology's embrace of positivism, which had important consequences for education, was the move towards reliance on statistical methods. In particular, the concept of the 'bell-shaped' or normal curve and the possibility of making comparisons between sample means have had a profound influence on educational method up to and including the present day. The origins of this technology in eugenics are of more than passing interest. Francis Galton, Darwin's cousin, was the first to apply the normal distribution in the 1860s. Both he and the statistician, Karl Pearson (and many others in the field), were active eugenicists. Eugenics was the science of improving the genetic quality of the stock which 'was born from a concern that the less intelligent sections of the population would breed more quickly than the more intelligent middle class sections and thus lower the overall intelligence in the population' (Olssen 1991: 190). The parallels here with evolutionary theory (ontogeny, phylogeny and inher-itance) are clear. So, too, is the influence, on *both* Darwinian evolution and the eugenics movement, of Malthus's prediction that a 'struggle for exist-ence' would ensue as population outstripped food supply. It was concerns such as these which led eugenicists to develop measures for classifying the mental abilities of the population and, via the bell-shaped curve, for equat-ing the *natural* of biological species and populations in their construction of the *normal* for human societies and samples.

Olssen (1991: 198) argues that the pervading feature of the various strands of psychology to emerge from these roots was that of 'methodological indi-vidualism': a model which could be traced through Hobbes, Locke and Descartes to a view of the individual person as 'self-moving, self-interested, pre-social, unitary, rational and a-historical'. This argument is maintained through the various accounts of the individual which different branches of psychology produced. For example, Freud's account saw the individual as a complex of biologically shaped drives which need to be repressed and constrained by society. Alternatively, cognitive development psychologies placed less emphasis on biology, but saw the individual as a unitary and rational actor with individual capacities which unfold according to inner mechanisms.

Behaviourism rejected biology altogether and emphasized the environmental determination of behaviour. In so doing, however, it still regarded the individual as distinct from culture, substituting a narrow definition of 'environment' for any consideration of social, cultural and structural factors (see Ingleby 1987). Behaviourists such as John Watson and, later, B. F. Skinner were among the most enthusiastic of those to embrace the positivist stance in psychology. Because anything to do with the mind or mental states (e.g. intentions, motives, meanings) could not be directly observed, they argued that only the observable behaviour of people could form the proper basis of study. What can be observed is what really counts, and what could be observed with respect to *learning* were stimulus-response and operant conditioning experiments with animals. The assumption of universal laws made learning a unitary phenomenon for study, and rendered unproblematic the interpretation and recasting of animal experiments into human learning and education. This led directly to the theories and practices of education which have been a vital part of the staff and educational development discourse, and which are considered in the following section.

Implications for educational and staff development

At the beginning of this chapter I posed a number of questions which staff developers sometimes encounter. These are unexceptional in that they appear to be reasonable questions for someone to ask and for which reasonable answers might be found. Very many more questions along these lines could be produced from the area of educational and staff development. But following from the discussion so far, the importance of the historical and intellectual milieux from which such questions arise should now be more apparent. In particular, the Enlightenment idea of progress through rationality is of crucial importance.

The Enlightenment period was one of optimism, of great discovery, of ever increasing explanation of the physical world, and of inexorable progress and upward advance as a fact of life. Individuals, constituted as separate, pre-social and naturally imbued with self-consciousness and critical rationality, would discover the inner logic of not only the physical world, but also social and moral development. The universal laws of human cognition and learning were conceived as real and attainable: out there waiting to be discovered. This would require specialization, however, and so it would come as no surprise to Max Weber, for example, that educational research professionals, followed by educational and staff development professionals, would emerge to shoulder the burden of explication of the inner nature of educational and staff development. Progress and development are natural and universal, and we have seen how the doctrine of positivism could guide us towards the discovery of educational knowledge. The importance of positivism for what staff developers do, and how they do it, has been immense, and its legacy is still with us. Indeed, it forms the basis for much of the advice developers give to practitioners with regard to how their students learn, and how they might teach.

The predominance of positivist educational psychology has led to reliance being placed upon results from seemingly innumerable empirical studies. In the main, these have compared one teaching method with another, under quasi-experimental (controlled) conditions. Such studies objectify both teachers and students as 'individual units', and accept instrumental values of 'efficient' or 'effective' teaching or learning as transcendent. Operationally, they tend to compare mean differences of performance by first-year students on 'objective' tests emphasizing factual recall, all of this occurring within a 'delivery of instruction' view of education. With the advent of meta-analysis, many such studies could be bundled together and analysed for overall 'effect size'. Thus one may learn, for example, that personalized instruction is more effective than lecturing (conventional teaching) (Kulik *et al.* 1979) and so, too, is computer-based teaching (Kulik *et al.* 1980).

In this kind of research are clearly evident the values which early psychology, especially eugenics and psychometrics, took from biology and evolutionary theory. Plants and animals 'naturally' form populations and species comprised of differentiated individuals which can be measured and ranked on various criteria. Of course the 'naturalness' of such taxonomies is illusory and its constructive nature is demonstrated particularly by temporal change. However, the 'natural' has been applied to student learning especially with regard to 'ability' (conceived as 'natural' ability) and later in terms of 'achievement'. Irrespective of what they are ranked on, students should come out as approximately normally distributed. If they do not, the assignment can be altered next time to produce a better result, or else the marks can be 'scaled' to conform to the *a priori* assumption.

Why small groups of people with different social, class, ethnic and gender experience should be expected to produce a normal distribution on each task is something of a mystery, unless the *normal* is being equated with the *natural*. But such an equation is contrary to the very idea of education, in that education assumes that outcomes are *produced*, they do not simply happen due to forces beyond our control. If there are students who do not understand something, it is our educational duty to help them with this and to assist their learning. There is no law of education which says that some should never understand, and that teachers are powerless to do anything about it. This is not to say that education cannot be or has not been conceived as a kind of modern eugenics movement – a system for sifting out the weaker so that the stronger or fitter might survive and flourish. It is instead to argue that there is nothing *natural* or *inevitable* about this view and that we can *choose* to take it or to dispute it.

This argument applies equally to staff development. Elements of the 'struggle for existence' analogy are now permeating teaching in higher education, especially as 'teaching' enters discussions on promotion. The ideas we use to govern our students can thus come to be used to govern their teachers. Empirical measures of teaching (usually though not inevitably based on student ratings) can be used to produce a (normal?) distribution and bandings of teaching performance. But there is nothing natural or inevitable about the ways in which we judge teaching performance. The distributions obtained from instruments measuring performance can be changed by changing the instruments. The 'natural' which is equated with the bell-shaped curve is but one possibility based upon a number of assumptions.

We see here the biological metaphor with its underlying assumptions being used to rank teachers, very often in terms of a vague idea of 'innate teaching ability'. Though many teachers themselves might accept that teachers are mostly born, rather than made, staff developers *have* to make the counter argument that 'remedial' action can be taken to improve the performance of those at the lower end of the distribution, and thus staff development is conceived as a process of remediation. Notice that as the distribution curve is an 'objective' view of reality, that it is 'natural' and simply what we find when we investigate, then the problem lies with individuals rather than the social environment in which they are located.

An alternative position would be to suggest that there is nothing natural about the conditions leading to teaching practices or performance and that to effect change one needs to change the conditions in which individuals find themselves. Notice also that there seems to be little question of what would happen if remedial staff development were successful: would the idea of a curve simply be abandoned, or would the norms be changed so that those gaining the lowest ranking would be in categories such as 'good' or 'very good'? The problem is to do with norm referencing as opposed to criterion referencing, and the degree to which each of these affects the other. In the assessment of student learning there has been a move away from norm referencing and predetermined failure rates and in favour of mastery- and competency-based learning. In terms of the evaluation of teaching, this would mean movement away from the idea of competition for ratings on a single scale as implied by the biological/psychometric model based on an equation of the natural and the normal. Instead we would need to imagine a distribution where all teachers could be expected to demonstrate competency, and a different model of reward in which continuing professional orientation towards excellence and innovation in teaching and learning would be valued. Such a model could encourage openness, cooperation and collegiality in the improvement of teaching and learning, rather than isolate and cast teachers into the competitive relationship they can experience at present. Ramsden (1992) has outlined aspects of this view of teaching evaluation as a natural professional consequence of teaching itself.

A similar point could be made with respect to the current fashion for 'league tables' of 'performance' on teaching and research. The legacy of Adam Smith and Malthus can clearly be seen in the 'objective' ranking of institutions or departments, the 'fittest' being rewarded with funding while the 'poorest' have the chance to shape up (without funding) or face the inevitable consequence of natural selection through competition. Again the point should be made that there is nothing inevitable in this at all; it is an ideological interpretation which can be challenged with regard to structural inequalities at the beginning of the exercise, the fact that the 'rules' or 'formulae' favour the already favoured, that redistribution is considered unimportant as is the possibility of working with criteria achieved by democratic process. This latter point also spills over into modern 'managerialism' in higher education generally, with its concern for control and the rationalization of organizations to improve effectiveness and efficiency. Again, there is nothing natural or inevitable about managerial control strategies, and nothing to preclude the espousal of greater democracy, participation or collegiality (see, for example, Moses, 1989; Smyth, 1989).

If we stay a little longer with the legacy that biology has provided for psychology, the area of learning theory deserves special attention. Theories of cognitive development could be seen as a way out of psychology's attempt to view learning as a singular phenomenon, based on animal conditioning experiments. For teachers uncomfortable with this notion of learning, and who claim that not all of their students learn in the same way, research into 'learning theory' and 'cognitive style' purports to provide answers necessary for effecting a match between student and task. Thus, famous classifications of learning have been constructed by Bloom *et al.* (1956) and by Gagné (1970), both claiming to describe types of learning ranging from the simple to the complex. These follow in the tradition of Piaget, who constructed a series of stages of intellectual development which he claimed all children follow in direct comparison with stages in their physical (biological) development. Not only that, but the stages of cognitive development follow the very course of scientific evolution itself.

It may well be that the psychological laws arrived at by means of our restricted method can be extended into epistemological laws arrived at by the analysis of the history of the sciences: the elimination of realism, of substantialism, of dynamism, the growth of relativism, etc. all these are evolutionary laws which appear to be common both to the development of the child and to that of scientific thought.

(Piaget 1960: 240)

Piaget's view of cognitive development has been severely criticized (Morss 1990; 1991) as part of the *biologizing of childhood*. There is no fixed, universal, unfolding and *progressive* sequence of cognitive development as suggested by Piaget. There is no necessary cognitive progression from the simple to the complex as suggested by taxonomies such as those of Bloom and Gagné (see Cherryholmes 1988; and Chapter 5 of this book). Similarly, the stages of moral development suggested by Piaget and amplified by Kohlberg, and suggested by Erikson, by Maslow, by Rokeach, by Freud, and for college education, by Perry, are equally suspect (see, for example, Collier *et al.* 1974). This needs some explanation.

Freud worked with a theory of recapitulation. He considered what are now thought of as modern neuroses to have once been normal human conditions. 'Oral' and 'anal' stages, recapitulate earlier animal stages, and neuroses experienced by the child are synonymous with those of the ancestor or the modern savage (see Gould 1977: 158). Neuroses are arrested development, and it is the purpose of psychoanalysis to complete the developmental progression. Freud also saw the history of civilization as recapitulated in the libidinal development of individuals. While this might seem a long way from educational development, one of the most popular books on group learning in use in higher educational development (Jaques 1984) offers Freudian notions and interpretations of introjection, projection and transference as helpful in understanding how groups work. The usefulness of such interpretations is debatable, but many would argue that Freud's equation of 'group' with the structure of the family as viewed by a patriarchal, bourgeois, Victorian gentleman falls a long way short of his claims to have uncovered 'essentials' of the psyche.

Perry's work is interesting in that it spanned 'intellectual and ethical' development, seeing these as progressing from absolutes such as 'we-right-good' (against 'others-wrong-bad'), through contextual relativism to a position whereby commitment in the light of multiple responsibilities is integrated with the affirmation of identity and expressed in the person's lifestyle (Perry 1970). Both Perry and Kohlberg appear to have been influenced by Erikson's conception of the developmental task of young adults as the resolution of personal identity and achievement with the interpersonal capacity for intimacy (Erikson 1968). There is thus much commonality in Perry's scheme and Kohlberg's three-stage model (from egocentric behaviour via role conformity towards autonomy) in which

[t]he most mature form of moral viewpoint is the universal ethical principle . . . where right is held to be defined by conscience in accord-

ance with one's own individual principles which appeal to logical comprehensiveness, universality, and self-consistency. Such principles are, as one might expect, abstract universal prescriptions rather than concrete moral rules like the ten commandments.

(Tomlinson 1974: 25)

It is not surprising that in developmental schemes such as these we once more return to echoes of the Enlightenment's 'good' and rational man. Stage theories do not give us a view of human nature, of learning or morality as *is*, but instead they give us a *normative* view from the perspective of their authors. With monotonous regularity, the highest point to be reached according to each stage theory is that which accords with the author's self-perception and cultural experience. The highest point of learning is usually to demonstrate intellectual control over the material world, obtained by processes synonymous with those of Western science. The end point is of necessity the stereotyped image of the culture-free, presumably white, middle-class, Western, male scientist/researcher: the mirror image of the author.

Feminist writers such as Gilligan (1982) have shown how women and women's experience have been excluded from models of psychological development. She has suggested how women (and men) need not hold the highest point of emotional or cognitive achievement as their dissociation from others in an individualistic competition for the achievement of autonomy, and how the building of relationships and nurturing of others may constitute an alternative perspective in constructing a high point for development. However, the high point of moral development according to psychology texts remains that which accords with the values of liberal, Western, middle-class men, and they are also the models of self-control with regard to what might otherwise be a rampant, male (Freudian) psyche. Whole societies may be held back from reaching the heights of development, just as whole generations of students may fail to attain the end point of cognitive or moral development, but these are simply aberrations in the progressive and historically inevitable evolution of societies and cognition. They are examples of arrested development, of stunted growth.

In order to reach the high points of attainment, we may have to recapitulate our earlier stages of evolutionary attainment, which ceased to be end points themselves at some time in the past. Now they are no more than building blocks towards our higher and ultimate destiny, and in fact it may be a good idea to build our curricula according to recapitulation theory, as Herbert Spencer suggested, and educational reformers such as Pestalozzi, Froebel and Herbart attempted to put into practice:

If there be an order in which the human race has mastered its various kinds of knowledge, there will arise in every child an aptitude to

acquire these kinds of knowledge in the same order ... Education
should be a repetition of civilization in little.

(Spencer 1861: 76 quoted in Gould 1977: 148)

The embryo metaphor of development as described in evolutionary recapitulation can thus be seen at work in much of our ordinary thinking about
the nature of education and educational development. *Learning* itself is seen
as being about the unfolding of sequential stages from 'low level' to 'high
level' and a predetermined end point.

In my own staff development activities I have organized sessions on lecturing where lecturers have been invited to demonstrate a continuum of
approaches to lecturing. At one end of this is didactic lecturing (just talking), but teachers should be encouraged to *develop* through this by introducing breaks, quizzes, buzz groups or any other of 53 interesting things
(see, for example, Gibbs *et al.* 1987). Moving still further along the continuum are case-based methods, reorganization of the curriculum into small-
group, problem-based activities, and finally self-directed learning and student
autonomy. In organizing such sessions, the embryo metaphor and recapitulation are clearly evident, in that their purpose can be interpreted as helping
to spur the arrested development of those attending towards their ultimate
transformation as fully developed teachers. When they reach that stage,
they will naturally have the same attitudes and orientation to teaching as
myself: as with all stage models, we see in the highest point of attainment
the mirror image of the writer.

When it comes to variation among students, although at least 19 cognitive styles have been described (Messick 1976), these often reduce to similar themes. Thus, for example, Witkin (1975) and Pask and Scott (1972),
although starting from different points and using differing methods, both
reached broadly similar conclusions concerning cognitive style. Students
may thus be ranged along a continuum from 'field-dependent' (holist,
global) to 'field-independent' (serialist, analytical) and the teacher's task
may be conceptualized as matching the type of activity to the type of student in the most efficient way possible.

This view of education as the 'delivery system' for effecting efficient means
in order to gain predetermined ends, is pervaded by instrumentalism. As
such, it fails to acknowledge the intrinsically value-laden nature of the relationship between means and ends in education. Our understandings of
the 'hidden curriculum' and of the 'medium as message' ought to suggest
that educational ends are anticipated in educational means. Thus, educational ends of improved problem-solving, critical thinking, skills in analysis,
synthesis, evaluation and so on, foreshadow and suggest means for attain-
ing these ends. For example, the unquestioned and passive acceptance of
lecture-based instruction, and the regurgitation of material in an examination, would appear to be inappropriate to such ends, as would instruction

'delivered' in the form of a page-turning computer-assisted learning 'tutor-ial', followed by a multiple-choice test calling for memorization.

For educational developers, the allure of positivist prescriptions for 'good' teaching practice is very tempting. How often have we answered questions or settled disputes with words such as 'the evidence suggests', 'most studies show' or 'that can be disproved by Smith's research which . . .', etc. We tend to cite the empirical research literature as a major source in establishing our legitimacy when dealing with 'clients'. Indeed, many times our clients approach us with these very demands, examples of which we have already seen at the beginning of this chapter. We know the literature tolerably well, whereas the client does not. We are thus able to appear authoritative and supply remarkably clear and concise answers. In so doing, we may skirt over some of the difficulties and be selective in our quoting of evidence, but after all, the clients are not experts in the field: they want simple, practical answers, rather than a review of the difficulties, problems and judgements involved.

But if we take the critiques of positivism to heart, there are many problems raised by our use of essentially positivistic empirical research. As we have seen, no matter how many empirical studies point in a particular direction with regard to educational practice, we can never *induce* from these a general law. Educational research is misconceived if it is seen as adding building blocks on the way to educational advance and the revelation of ultimate truths. We are not in the business of erecting ever more truthful propositions upon secure foundational knowledge. Indeed, if we proceed by trying to 'discover' the 'natural' 'laws' which should govern educational practice, then we have to accept that such natural laws are beyond contes-tation. In so doing, we constrain ourselves to the present historical and social articulation of these laws, and thus to working within the status quo of educational practice, and adopting a conservative orientation. Popper and Kuhn's critiques have shown the provisional nature of the knowledge we produce, the *critical* rather than foundational nature of research, the possibility of radical change, and the importance of the metaphysical and *a priori* in our constitution and interpretation of the 'facts' which we generate from research. In particular, the theory impregnation of empirical obser-vation is a major item which should cause us concern. In Chapter 5 this will be further elaborated with respect to notions of 'deep' and 'surface' approaches to learning, but the consequences of supposedly 'value-neutral' observation are widespread.

For example, as staff developers we may be called upon to observe a col-league's lectures and offer advice. In so doing, we are not 'simply observ-ing' but observing, constructing and interpreting a small part of the domain of possibilities in accordance with our implicit theories of what is important and what should be done. Where do these come from? They come from the experience which has shaped our understanding, including, for example, books we have read on the areas in which we are interested, such as what comprises an exemplary lecturing style. Interesting though these may be, they are themselves predicated on what the authors consider appropriate, often according to a certain amount of their own empirical research. And the origins of such research usually reach back to the same psychology which has been touched upon a number of times already. Thus, the advice that we should open a lecture with something imaginative and stimulating comes from animal learning experiments where 'set induction' (making ready, preparing) often results in the improved performance of a rat in navigating a maze, which is called 'learning'. Giving an outline of what will be covered in the lecture (an 'advanced organizer') comes in part from cognitive development theory whereby we are supposedly better able to cope with new information if we have an idea of where it fits in with our pre-existing, presumably stable, usually tree-like (pre-hypertext) 'cognitive structures'. Giving an outline at the beginning, an elaboration and a sum-mary at the end also fits in with the repetition which again improves the performance of animals in 'learning' experiments. Advice to move from the simple and concrete to the complex echoes themes from recapitulation, evolution and cognitive psychology. We must always try to 'positively rein-force' 'correct' behaviour: food pellets for good (fast) animal performance. We should use 'visuals' such as overhead projector transparencies, slides and videos because 90% of sensory information processed by the brain comes through the eyes: neuro-physiological and psychological perception experiments. We should not lecture for more than half an hour at a time but have a break because of 'attention span': very limited physiological experimentation plus suggestions that this is a good idea.

I am not suggesting that any of these exhortations is necessarily bad, but I *am* pointing out how the discourse of psychology could mould our obser-vation of a teaching activity and guide our prescriptions for better prac-tice. Personally, however, I find a view of education as something which can be 'done' to essentially passive but manipulable individuals (as in animal experiments) woefully inadequate as a foundation for human learning.

In the courses we mount for new staff, we may thus cite positivist studies of what makes a 'good' lecturer, what is an exemplary lecturing style or, in a slightly modified form, what is good lecturing in a particular discipline. We have empirical justification for what is more effectively accomplished in a lecture as opposed to a tutorial. In tutorials, there is a great deal of empirical data on who speaks for how long and what they say. We even have recommendations as to the optimum number of students in a tutorial group. Again, the theory dependence of the observations from which our prescrip-tions are born is seldom mentioned. If we make a category analysis of a colleague's tutorials, then, we are simply reporting what happened: teacher talk, student talk, initiation, response, etc. It is the real world we are observ-ing and these are the facts.

If we accept this kind of knowledge as providing a model for what is good and bad in teaching *behaviours*, we can mount video-taped micro teaching sessions for people to practise their behaviours until they get them 'right'. This approach may also spill over into the area of individual consultation, where we might see ourselves as objective professionals or technicians, fine-tuning the teaching (technical) behaviours of a particular client. In so doing, we concentrate on observable behaviours and changing such behaviours according to empirical research evidence and accepted prescriptions. The individual teacher's own value positions are irrelevant in this, as it is purely a technical problem of skill development.

Similarly, where there are problems or questions to be investigated, we assist in the development of empirical data gathering methods and a research design. Until recently, educational research has been dominated by positivist psychology, which is 'more widely published, taught, accepted, and rewarded in educational research circles than any other approach' (Rist 1977: 42, quoted in Candy 1991: 430–31). This applies equally to adult education (Boud 1983) and the many other branches of education. Because of this, my suspicion is that most of us who are staff developers have at least some background in educational psychology rather than, for example, educational or social theory and philosophy. This becomes apparent when we look at the literature on educational development. Thus, in Clarke's (1981) bibliography of educational development we find six pages of references devoted to 'educational theory' compared with 24 on 'educational media' and 175 pages of references in total. Beard *et al.* (1978) catalogue many, mainly positivist studies, under chapter headings of 'Aims and Objectives', 'Economy and Efficiency', 'Recall and Retention of Information', 'Skills and Abilities', 'Teaching for Change of Attitudes' and 'Evaluation of Students, Teachers and Teaching Methods'. While lamenting that educational research has not been as rigorous as research in some of the natural sciences, they are confident that the use of better *experimental* designs and the statement of results in probabilistic terms will provide more secure building blocks upon which to construct a better science of education and improved teaching:

> Since ... by no means all educational experiments are rigorously designed, some tend to reject the results altogether. But, in doing so, they discard the few sound beginnings in scientific method which have so far been made in the educational field and revert to attitudes and subjective judgements appropriate to a pre-scientific era. The remedies lie in more widespread use of good designs in educational experiments as well as appreciation on the part of teachers that results of experiments which are stated only in terms of probabilities may yet have value in guiding policies or in the selection of teaching methods.
>
> (Beard *et al.* 1978: 2)

It is natural, therefore, that in the research *and* consultation area there is a strong pressure to reproduce the positivist orientation which we have absorbed and which much of the research literature has promoted. This is not a trivial point, as so often considerations of educational, staff or professional development are cast in the 'here and now', dissociated from tradition, ideology or epistemology. But we are part of a tradition and a deeply embedded part of that tradition includes a notion of development.

A conception of development links our current endeavours to the broad historical, social and intellectual themes which characterized the rise of science, and particularly its manifestation in evolutionary theory and psychology, throughout the eighteenth, nineteenth and twentieth centuries. Use of the word 'development' thus brings with it much that we could do without.

> Staff development is a term I dislike and rarely use. Educators have borrowed it from biology where it is used as a synonym for (but often not quite coextensive with) ontogeny. Into this precise meaning they mix a vague and variable mish-mash of maturation, adaptation, and 'improvement' ... it would be best if we got rid of the term in the context of university teaching.
>
> (Quoted in Matheson 1981: 157)

One of the central messages of this book is that 'development' is a site for contestation – it is not a unitary concept which we will one day provide a model for. The very meaning of the word, how it is constituted, what kinds of activity it implies, are all discursive, and can be interpreted according to various ontological and epistemological standpoints. There is no super-standard from which we can judge these positions, our notions of development are of necessity a site for encounter and dispute. We have to break the link of development with the natural, with evolution, with growth, with a unitary notion of progress, all of which suppress the contestable nature of development and make it seem inevitable and good.

One of the definitions given earlier in this chapter (with respect to evolution) referred to '*growing* as opposed to *being made*'. We need to stand this view on its head with regard to development, and acknowledge that we *choose* what we mean by development, and the kind of development we wish to pursue. A view of development as natural, progressive and good is not helpful in this respect. If we accept the phylogenic message of evolution, rather than the embryo metaphor, then we may view development as having no preordained end point, no predetermined direction, no preplanned purpose and no necessary stages along the way. This is a fundamentally different stance to the positions which have been outlined in this chapter.

The age of progress is now over and we need to announce the death of development. As we will see in the following chapters of this book, many people have come to this realization and there has recently been much rewriting of the development stories which were hitherto foundational to our thinking. Prising development away from 'naturalness' and replacing it with humanity and constructiveness is now an urgent task. Why? To quote Morss (1993):

> Development is a story with which we clothe ourselves. It is a technique for setting a ... distance between oneself and another, that is, of categorising the other as a less mature version of oneself. It says to the other that here is a path which we share and on which I am ahead: 'I am your future: you will become (like) me.'

In a recent paper entitled 'Announcing the death of development, again', I posed a number of questions for educational and staff developers. It is perhaps appropriate to quote the final passage as a way of closing this chapter:

> If you are a staff developer, try thinking about your dealings with the people you 'develop.' How 'equal' is this relationship and how do you attempt to privilege your own view of the world? What developmental notion are you pushing and is the high point of development someone just like yourself? What stages do you see people going through to become like you and how do you go about creating the recapitulation of your own progression in others? Then think that your message is wrong.

(Webb 1993: 104)

3

Staff Development for Understanding People and Ourselves

... understanding is the primordial mode of being of what we most essentially are ... It is not just one activity which is to be distinguished from other human activities, but underlies all human activities.

(Bernstein 1983: 144)

Introduction

'Staff development' is concerned with people. Even using the word 'staff' tends to objectify the flesh and blood human beings who *are* staff. The word may be used for this very purpose. 'Staff' signifies an objective unity, common aim and intent, as opposed to the emotion, feeling, difference and idiosyncrasy which we experience with 'people'. To engage in 'people development' is considered by some to be arrogant and unacceptable. For example, Matheson (1981: 155) reports the views of one of his respondents as follows:

> I am still wary of the notion that staff can/should be 'developed' as people. Many of my academic colleagues would regard efforts to change *them* as impertinent ... I realise that this is a restricted view, but it is a fact that activities focussing on knowledge and skills in an impersonal way are more acceptable 'staff development' than overt attempts to 'facilitate your personal growth.'

This person sees staff development as a technical process of 'knowledge and skills' development, improving techniques without altering in any profound sense the humanity or Being of a person. Neither would the staff developer be altered to any great extent, the relationship being neutral and professional, with a specific technical focus. It is a view of staff development encountered in the previous chapter, with the focus on what claims to be a neutral and scientific view of development and progress based on positive knowledge.

This view does not adequately describe my own experience of educational and staff development, nor of learning. In my experience the feelings,

emotions and 'humanity' of the people involved have played an important part in the educational or staff development encounter. We have often
started out with very different interpretations of the world and human
nature, the purpose of teaching, attitudes towards students and so on. As
we have worked together in a staff development relationship we have
developed a rapport beyond the technical task at hand. The technical task
may have been improving an individual's lecturing (following poor student
evaluations, for example), introducing problem-based learning, increasing
student participation in small-group discussions and so on. But as the relationship has grown and we have sought to understand each other better,
we have each had to change and adjust our views. We have attempted to
extend our horizons and glimpse what it is like to see the world from the
standpoint of another human being. The learning which has taken place
has engaged the people involved at the personal and emotional level: it has
become personally important for them. In other relationships, of course,
none of this has happened.

Many staff developers would claim that 'understanding people' is fundamental to what they do and what they can achieve. Because they work
with people from many different contexts, staff developers often gain repu-
tations for being 'understanding people' themselves. They can be called
in to facilitate difficult meetings, to guide departmental retreats, to act as
go-betweens when staff and students are having difficulties over a particular issue. In Warren Piper's Model B category, they may facilitate strategic
planning and policy formation workshops at various organizational levels.
They are good 'process people'. But while staff developers may talk freely
with each other about this 'human relationship' side of their work, it does
not tend to have a high profile in their academic writings. It seems to be
taken for granted. When initiatives to introduce problem-based learning,
or better small-group discussions, or better lecturing come to be written up,
the human side of a staff development relationship seldom comes through.
We have theories of learning and teaching, practical techniques and prescriptions, but seldom any insight into the *personal* nature of the process
from which the abstractions are drawn. This chapter traces some strands in
the legitimation of human understanding and the importance of human
relationships. It seeks to paint humanity back into the staff development
picture.

The wing-footed messenger

Hermes was the wing-footed messenger-god who delivered the messages of
the gods to the mortals of the human world. He not only *announced* messages
but also acted as *interpreter*. In so doing he might clarify, add to or comment
upon the message, in order to render it intelligible, and to ensure that

mortals understood what it meant. Interestingly, the Greeks credited Hermes with the origination of language and writing, 'the tools which human understanding employs to grasp meaning and to convey it to others' (Palmer 1969: 13). Language and writing form the bases for human understanding and they have thus played an important part in the growth of the 'Hermes tradition' or hermeneutics, as it came to be called.[1] The essence of the Hermes or hermeneutical tradition has been to ensure that 'something foreign, strange, separated in time, space, or experience is made familiar, present, comprehensible; something requiring representation, explanation, or translation is somehow "brought to understanding" – is "interpreted"' (Palmer 1969: 14). From the earliest times the usefulness of 'bringing to understanding' the important texts, writings and traditions of society was recognized. The Greek educational system taught literary interpretation and criticism with regard to Homer and the later poets, and when the Renaissance rediscovered classical writings, interpretation, discussion and criticism received a boost as 'ancient wisdom' became not only a model for artistic and scientific education, but for living 'the good life' (Bleicher 1980).

Interpretative activity also continued to follow the Hermes tradition in the exegesis (commentary, clarification, explanation) of religious texts. Rabbis developed rules for the interpretation of the Talmud and Midraschim, but for biblical hermeneutics the Reformation demanded a dramatic change of direction. Whereas the Catholic Church emphasized the power of the hierarchy and of tradition in the interpretation of Scriptures, Protestantism claimed that, in principle, biblical understanding was open to *anyone* using a universal hermeneutical method. At the core of this method was the belief that the interpretation of any part of a text could only be determined by considering it in terms of the intent and form of the whole. But this obviously raised the question: 'what *was* the intent of the writer?' The question was equally important in law, leading to the development of juridical hermeneutics. Judges and lawyers need to establish the intention of the law-maker or codifier before they can apply the law to the variety of particular cases which confront them. A systematic account of hermeneutics was needed.

Circles of understanding

Schleiermacher, writing in the late eighteenth and early nineteenth centuries, proposed a universal system for the interpretation not just of legal documents, Scriptures and works of literature, but for utterances and texts of all kinds. His system conceived of two aspects of interpretation: the grammatical and psychological. For the grammatical he developed 44 'canons', the two most important being as follows. First, a particular piece of text can only be interpreted with reference to the language shared by the original author and his or her public. Second, the meaning of each word must be determined with reference to the words which surround it (see Bleicher 1980).

A similar emphasis on the importance of viewing each part in terms of the whole was found in the psychological sphere, too. Here, the interpreter needs to investigate and understand the emergence of thought within the totality of the author's life and experiences. This having been accomplished, it is possible that the translator or interpreter may bring to consciousness things of which even the original author may have remained unconscious. In so doing, as Dilthey (1958, XIV/I: 707) later observed, the person under-taking the interpretation may come to understand the original author 'bet-ter than he had understood himself' (quoted in Bleicher 1980: 15).

Schleiermacher represents the beginning of a modern understanding of hermeneutics in his linking of philology (the 'science' of interpretation regarding language and grammatical structures) with the 'art' of psycho-logical understanding, especially with regard to empathy in the relationship between interpreter and author. The hermeneutical task is made neces-sary because of separateness – for example, the separation in time or space of author and interpreter (or, more generally, the 'Other'). The greater the empathy, affinity and communion of perspective which the interpreter can share with the 'Other', the more accurate will be the interpretative account rendered. Hermeneutics is thus much more than a technical, prac-tical or mechanical concern: 'the foundational act of all hermeneutics [is] the act of understanding, the act of a living, feeling, intuiting human being' (Palmer 1969: 85).

Schleiermacher is also responsible for clearly describing the paradoxical nature of understanding, and this is of fundamental educational importance. He termed this paradox the 'hermeneutical circle', and it can be used at many different levels and in many different areas. On a personal note, I have found the notion of the hermeneutical circle to be among the most useful of tools in attempting to illuminate educational and staff development situations. I will therefore take a little time to outline and illustrate what it means.

A good example of an hermeneutic circle is found in the way we attempt to understand a sentence. We can only understand the meaning of a sentence by understanding the meaning of each individual word. This could result in the reductive (scientific) position that if we understand each small constituent part, we will understand the whole. Yet at the same time, indi-vidual words have many interpretations and functions. If we look up each word in a dictionary we are offered a number of alternative explanations and equivalents. It is argued that the meaning of a *particular* word in a particular context is given by its place in the sentence, and by reference to the meaning of the sentence *as a whole*. The paradox of the hermeneut-ical circle is that we cannot understand the meaning of the whole without understanding the meaning of each of the parts, and yet we will never know the meaning of a particular part without first having a grasp of the meaning of the whole.

And the problem does not end there. A similar point may also be made with respect to *all* knowledge:

A 'fact' does not stand on its own independent from its context or its interpreter, but rather is partially constituted by them. A fact can be evaluated only in relation to the larger structure of theory or argument of which it is a part. At the same time, this larger structure is dependent on its individual parts, as well as on other related information. In explicating the circle of understanding, we move back and forth between part and whole.

(Woolfolk *et al.* 1988: 7)

Much educational theorizing has been bipolar. For example, students may be 'field-dependent' or 'field-independent', 'global' or 'analytical', 'serialist' or 'holist', 'deep' or 'surface' orientated. An exam may be answered by 'rote learning' or by 'analytical' or 'critical' reasoning. Relationships have also been seen as hierarchical, linear and causal. For example, 'knowledge' is a necessary but inferior precursor to 'comprehension', which in turn precedes 'application', followed by 'analysis', 'synthesis' and 'evaluation'. And in an equally linear fashion, the role of a staff developer may be to observe the behaviour of a lecturer, diagnose what is going wrong and suggest a new strategy. Or again, teaching may be analysed and reduced to specific behaviours which can be improved by repetition in micro teaching situations. The insight of the hermeneutical circle allows a somewhat different view.

As learners we may be both one thing and another, constantly moving between positions. In order to gain a global understanding of a concept, we may have to reduce it to its elements, to label, to take it apart, to analyse. As we do this we learn more about the element, but also gain a new perspective on the whole concept. Alternatively, we might make a single intuitive leap to a grasp of the concept as a whole, perhaps through the application of a metaphor or analogy from elsewhere. We are then better able to locate and appreciate a particular element within the overall concept. Most often, we continually shift from part to whole and from whole to part, in attempting to enrich our understanding. This means that it does not matter *where* one enters a circle of understanding, the important thing is the subtlety of the relationship and the constant shifting of position between part and whole.

In staff development this movement between part and whole is played out time and again. A lecturer (suppose it is a man) is reluctant to have students in a lecture class discuss a problem in pairs for a few moments before asking for comment. He acknowledges that it could help students to marshal their ideas, that students can learn from each other in such a discussion, that it will convey a message that it is acceptable to talk in class and that this may make students less reticent to contribute when the lecturer asks general questions. Why is he so reluctant?

In discussing this with the lecturer, a staff developer (suppose it is a woman) slowly learns more about the lecturer. Although not appearing to be at all nervous, he is in fact terrified of the class. He is frightened that they will ask questions he is unable to answer. He sees them as antagonistic and waiting for him to make a mistake, which they will then pounce upon with great delight. He claims some experience of this having happened in the past and relates an example. The lecturer goes on to describe how he is quite insecure about a number of things in his life, and the staff developer interprets this insecurity as leading to a fear of relinquishing even the smallest amount of control in class.

What might at first have appeared to be a small and simple (technical/practical) suggestion is now seen in a broader context. The staff developer may argue for the effectiveness of the suggestion or even offer definitive research evidence in its favour. All to no avail. The practical suggestion is not being considered on the same scale of effectiveness or rationality. The staff developer needs to understand this, but that in itself is not possible unless the relationship between herself and the lecturer has reached a point where confidences can be shared. Let us suppose that this happens; as they talk more comfortably with each other, the lecturer admits that he has always found the staff developer to be somewhat intimidating. She is so relaxed, at ease and confident: she gets on so well with everyone. He feels inadequate and threatened by her and this increases his reluctance to 'give away' anything about himself. The staff developer is amazed at this revelation and goes on to explain that she has to work very hard at getting on with people and that she often feels inadequate and intimidated herself. She explains how she had heard of the research and publication record of the lecturer and how she was herself somewhat overawed by his reputation as they started the process. What has happened, therefore, is that she, too, has expanded her horizon of understanding and of self-understanding: she has come to realize something about herself.

Both participants in the relationship have been changed by it. From the staff developer's standpoint, it is now possible to interpret the (part) behaviour and attitude of the lecturer because she has been given access to more privileged knowledge (of the whole). What will happen as a result of this? Perhaps nothing at all. On the other hand, perhaps the lecturer is dissatisfied with what he increasingly sees as the consequences of his insecurity, and he wants to make some changes. He moves from the whole to the part once more and recognizes the importance of trying pair discussions in class. This small device has assumed a symbolic status representing a larger wish to overcome his insecurity and relate better to the class, and to people more generally. He tries the pair discussion and survives. With a new confidence he tries other changes. His confidence grows still further and he makes changes in his life outside of the classroom. The initial, trivial, technical suggestion of a staff developer has had a dramatic effect upon a person's life and being. This has come about by the building of a relationship between two people, which has changed both. It has also been made possible by the interpretation of the particular within the whole and the whole within the particular, back and forth. If this kind of inter-pretative method could be systematized, then we could conceive of a truly human science.

Human science

Schleiermacher died in 1834, a year after the birth of Wilhelm Dilthey. Dilthey (who became Schleiermacher's biographer) would adapt Schleier-macher's insight for a much grander purpose. In short, Dilthey sought to found a new science of human and social understanding which would stand in opposition to the positivism of the natural sciences.

The roots of a science expressly for human and social understanding pre-date Dilthey and may be traced to Giambattista Vico's pioneering work, *New Science*, of 1725. Vico argued that the social world, since it is of hu-man creation, is in principle more intelligible than the natural world. At its crudest, Vico's argument is that human beings, in their interrogation of the natural world, will never have the ultimate confirmation of their explana-tions which would be afforded by a molecule being able to say, for example: 'yes, I understand and accept your explanation of me.' Such confirmation is only conceivable in the human world, in terms of human and social act-ivity, and, at its base, in the possibility of the understanding of one human being by another.

Dilthey followed this line of reasoning, but combined it with the her-meneutical insights and methods of Schleiermacher. In so doing he was embracing the German romantic tradition of, for example, Novalis and Goethe and reacting against the realism, reductionism and objectification of positive science. Science was viewed as static, mechanical, causal, law-bound, and functioning with abstract categories such as number, space and time. In opposition to this, Dilthey (and other 'life' philosophers) stressed the immediacy, intuitiveness, uniqueness, passion and emotion of the lived experience of human beings.

In essence, Dilthey was seeking a fusion of the two great strains of Euro-pean philosophy: Anglo-French empiricism, rationalism and positivism, and German idealism and romanticism. His quest for a human science thus sought to reconcile a need for 'objectively valid' data, while at the same time retaining the immediacy and authenticity of lived human experience.

In contrast to the natural or physical sciences (*Naturwissenschaften*), he used the term *Geisteswissenschaften* to indicate human sciences in which *Geist*, the human mind or spirit, could be objectively studied and understood. And the object of the human sciences should not be to understand life in terms of a natural science with categories extrinsic to it, but from the intrinsic categories used by human beings and derived from life itself.

Dilthey noted how in the veins of the rational and reasoning 'knowing subject' of Enlightenment philosophers such as Locke, Hume and Kant, 'runs no real blood' (Dilthey 1958, V: 4), and how 'knowing' had become synonymous with 'thinking' and separated from feeling, willing, wanting, and the cultural and historical life experiences which shape our thoughts and actions. Because its subject comprises meanings, purposes, plans, goals and intentions as opposed to non-intentional events, the human sphere of study is different in kind to that of the physical sciences. So, where natural science may seek explanation (*Erklären*) of nature, human science should seek understanding (*Verstehen*) of human life, the kind of understanding which only one human being can show for the life experiences of another.[2]

As a means of achieving *Verstehen*, Dilthey made life itself – the concrete, historical and lived experience of human beings – the centre of attention. In order to gain access to life or lived experience, the interpreter needs to 'relive' in an empathic way the life, culture and times of the person (object or text) of which understanding is sought. In his earlier writings he thus placed much emphasis upon intuitively trying to understand the psychological states and intentions of the Other. He gradually moved away from this psychological account, however, and towards a more 'objective' expression of the cultural and historical environment within which writings or artefacts were created. But it always remained his position that *Verstehen* could only take place because, as human beings, our own mental experiences allow us to appreciate those of another. Dilthey always viewed *Verstehen* as a conversational kind of process in which the interpreter would learn by adjusting his or her perspective and understanding. In entering the inner world of the Other, there appears 'the possibility of finding in another person the profound depths of our own experience; from the encounter can come the discovery of a fuller inner world' (Palmer 1969: 104). One discovers and rediscovers oneself in the Other. *Verstehen* is therefore not simply a cognitive or intellectual procedure for understanding the Other, but instead a realization in terms of *all* our mental processes and life experiences. These include our emotional and intuitive understandings, forged in the perennial human riddles of life and death, joy and sorrow, love and hate, the value of an individual life, and its meaninglessness. In short, *Verstehen* understanding anticipates a completeness and richness which follow from human experience, which surpass rational explication, and which have importance for both parties.

The consequences of conceiving staff development relationships along these lines are both profound and commonplace. They are profound in terms of legitimizing a 'whole-person' approach to staff development relationships, which in turn opens up richer and wider possibilities than would otherwise be the case. They are also profound in terms of the possibility for mischief, in the hands of a staff developer with manipulative, exploitative or abusive intent.

But the consequences are commonplace, too. As staff developers and teachers we routinely use our own experiences of 'what it was like to be a student' or 'what I have experienced as a lecturer' in order to comprehend and understand the experiences of others. Indeed, we may often find it easier and more comfortable to reinterpret the expressions of others in terms of our own experiences. It is perhaps in the areas of being more open to the experiences of others, and of re-evaluating and reinterpreting our own experiences, that many of us need help.

While these insights remain with us today, other aspects of Dilthey's work seem constrained by the times in which he was writing. He moved gradually from seeking psychological understanding of a particular Other, and towards seeking a historical and social basis for understanding more generally. But he did so patchily. For example, he had no historical, social or contextual view of the natural sciences. So while placing the human sciences firmly within a framework of historical and social understanding, he still retained the wish that they should produce a rigorous 'objectively valid knowledge', of a similar kind to that which the natural sciences were then thought to produce. In this he reflected the scientistic attitudes of his time. But his locating of human understanding within a historical and social framework, rather than an atemporal and aspatial (supposedly scientific) one, provided the opportunity for Martin Heidegger to explore the nature of *self*-understanding.

Self-understanding

Like Dilthey, Heidegger also wanted a way of 'disclosing life' in its own terms. But unlike Dilthey, he was not concerned with a theory of knowledge (epistemology) or a methodology for the human sciences: his quest was for a knowledge which preceded these, for a theory of what *is*, before we even begin to construct our ideas about the world, society or the nature of knowledge. This is the domain of ontology.

He started by reversing the Western metaphysical tradition which had developed through Kant and Descartes, and which held that as thinking subjects we conceive, construct and impose ideas upon the world we experience. A counter-position to this is that 'things themselves', or phenomena, show themselves to us. A thing is what it is before we come to build our conscious verbal and written schemes and categories for describing and capturing it. This is the basis of 'phenomenology', that is, being led by things to an understanding of them in their own terms. The idea of phenomenology had been developed by Heidegger's teacher, Edmund Husserl, who thought that a rigorous scientific method for reaching such understanding might be accomplished. He believed that the artefacts of human creation could be traced back towards the human consciousness of their development, and that consciousness laid open or exposed. A good example of this lies in his essay investigating the origins of geometry as a human artefact, reprinted as Husserl (1978).[3]

Heidegger did not ground understanding in human consciousness or the categories which we construct to capture phenomena, but in the reality or 'manifestness' of the things themselves. Grasping this reality produces a somewhat different form of *Verstehen*.

'Understanding' for Schleiermacher emphasized the importance of merging oneself with the Other, while Dilthey emphasized the need to interpret human social and psychological artefacts as expressions of 'inner realities' and of 'life' itself. For Heidegger 'understanding' is not the nurturing of human empathy, nor is it gaining a deeper grasp of a human activity. Understanding is not something to be possessed or developed. It is simply a part of our being, or, as Heidegger would say, our being-in-the-world. It is that part of our being which recognizes or is conscious of our *own* being. His word for this is *Dasein* (from *da* meaning 'there' and *sein* meaning 'being'). 'There-being' is fundamental, and prior to every act of thought and expression, every act of existing. Every human being has always found himself or herself already immersed in the world, a world of experience with its preconceived understandings already in place. We are always already in the world, and 'world' is prior to any conceptualizing we may do about it. This includes conceptualizing that the subjective self is separate from an objective world. Concepts such as 'subjective' and 'objective', 'self' and 'world', only come after there-being.

'Understanding' also has a prestructure as it is conducted through language, and language itself shapes how things are viewed and carries its own interpretative leanings. Understanding is thus always already embedded in the world, always already interpreting, and always subject to presuppositions, predeterminations and prejudices.

> The hope of interpreting 'without prejudice and presupposition' ultimately flies in the face of the way understanding operates. What appears from the 'object' is what one allows to appear and what the thematization of the world at work in his understanding will bring to light. It is naive to assume that what is 'really there' is 'self-evident.' The very definition of what is presumed to be self-evident rests on a body of unnoticed presuppositions, which are present in every

interpretive construction by the 'objective' and 'presuppositionless' interpreter.

(Palmer 1969: 136)

There are similarities here with the theory-impregnated nature of observation discussed in Chapter 2, and also problems for phenomenologists and phenomenographers who hope 'simply' to observe and describe either phenomena or concepts.

Heidegger goes behind Western thinking to the questions which give rise to the Western tradition, in order to draw out meanings which have remained hidden. Preunderstanding is responsible for providing a context in which an object subtly comes to be ordered. Western preunderstanding orders with regard to the demands of logical and conceptual thought. Truth thus becomes 'correct seeing and thinking', a matter of placing an idea before the mind's eye, as it were, so that ideas may then be 'properly' manipulated. To use Rorty's (1979) pregnant phase, mind and the philosophy it constructs become the 'mirror of nature'.

In the Western philosophical system, the subject (person) conceives an object, and names and manipulates it for the subject's benefit. Science reigns supreme as serving the subject's will to master. However, art objects also become objectifications of a person's values, objectifications of human experience. Values serve as no more than a stop-gap to give 'things' some meaning back, since this is lost when subjects conceive of things as objects. Any sense of sacredness or of value independent of human beings, is inconceivable. The status of things is reduced to their usefulness to people, and people are the centre and measure of all. Thinking is thus conceived in terms of control over objects and experience, of mastery and exploitation, rather than of open responsiveness to the world and of conservation. But hermeneutics can go behind the Western metaphysic to bring out hidden meaning, revelation and disclosure. This is the hermeneutical task for philosophy and more generally for all acts of interpretation.

Heidegger has thus moved a very long way from the view of hermeneutics as a conceptual, objective, technical act of analysis, *or* a means for gaining a deeper appreciation of a shared humanity through empathy. Truth and understanding are always already there in the world. It is our duty to bring this out of concealment and thus make truth a concrete, historical fact. Hermeneutics is the process by which the understanding which is always already there is brought to light, and thus to manifest existence.

There are insights here for staff developers. As humans we are beings aware of our own being; we are beings-in-the-world before all else. This puts our humanity centre-stage, rather than marginalizing it into an awkward 'randomness' or 'variability'. Heidegger speaks of 'care' for people, which fits quite comfortably with humanistic psychology and educational notions of growth, development, freedom, self-direction and autonomy. Care indicates an acknowledgment of the sacredness of people and things. They have value and should be honoured in their own right. But how difficult this is! We have views of teaching and learning which we think are right. We truly believe that self-directed learning or peer assessment are good. We believe our view of biculturalism, multiculturalism, liberalism, feminism, post-structuralism or class politics is right and important for educational practices. We attempt to defeat alternative views by the force and rhetorical skill of our argument. Usually, we want to win, rather than to understand.

In staff development seminars considering case studies of teaching (for examples of these, see Schwartz and Webb 1993) I have seen teachers amazed by the differing interpretations their colleagues have of what for them seem perfectly clear situations. I have been amazed myself, and occasionally shocked, by what I consider to be a reactionary attitude to students or teaching. I have seen people speak past each other on these occasions and many others. I have seen those articulating a particular kind of feminism, cultural sensitivity or class politics, be antagonistic towards and dismissive of alternative views to their own. I have also observed liberal rationalists show little conception of the emotional content often involved in feminist, cultural or class arguments. I have adopted various of these positions myself, and conceived it my duty to have others adopt them, too. Similarly, I have been persuaded by a particular view of learning or education and then sought to propagate it with vigour. In so doing I have often suspended my human faculty for seeking understanding and instead become determined to win. In dealing with people, hermeneutics can remind us of some of the consequences of our actions. Learning that true understanding is rarely developed through spiteful dismissal or crushed argument is a long and painful process. But as staff developers, we need to maintain our relationships with people. The world changes, people change, new arguments come forward, there are new points to discuss. Maintaining a relationship makes this possible.

At times I have been involved in staff development relationships which have changed and educated both parties. We, the people involved, have come to a better understanding of a particular problem, partly through a better understanding of each other. We have learned where we disagree and for what reasons. But we have also developed a unique common understanding of the problem. In the case studies seminars mentioned above, in teaching consultations, in institutional research projects concerning teaching and learning, persistent themes from my own life and from the lives of those I work with are played out in unique situations. There is no single method to follow in all of this, no rule to apply, and after so many years it is disconcerting to think that one is starting from scratch, yet again. However, if our staff development activities are to be 'life'-based and not formulaic, then this is as it should be. Staff development, under this view, is a dialogical activity: it is staff development by conversation: 'The keys to understanding are not manipulation and control but participation and openness, not knowledge but experience, not methodology but dialectic' (Palmer 1969: 215).

Truth and method

The image of 'flesh and blood' human beings becomes lost in Heidegger's writings as he attempts to 'think Being without beings' (DiCenso 1990: 77). The lure of atemporal and ahistorical revelation, as ever, proves irresistible. But the Hermes tradition continues and has most recently been reworked by Heidegger's student, Hans-Georg Gadamer. The title of Gadamer's major work, *Truth and Method* (1975), encapsulates the direction of much of the content: that truth cannot be achieved by an objective method.

There are some important lessons for educational and staff developers in Gadamer's work. For example, he uses the example of how people regard a great work of art to illustrate the reversal of 'method-driven' enquiry. He claims that interpretation of an object, a situation, another person, is not about the questioner using methods to gain understanding. This leads to the questioner controlling and manipulating the event. Our reaction to a great work of art is the opposite of this in that the work itself opens up to us a richer world. Through the work of art we come better to appreciate the world, our being in it and our own self-understanding. We are not interrogating the work of art, it is putting the question to us: 'what is our self-understanding?'

I see some parallels here with teaching. We all know from our own experiences that good teachers we have encountered (artists, as it were), have done more than present content material. In good teachers, the content material and the process of teaching come together in the *person* of the teacher. Good teachers bare aspects of their Being by sharing their experience of existence and humanity. Students sitting in a lecture may want to 'get down the facts', but they also learn much about the teacher as a human being. It is often aspects of the person which are remembered years after the subject matter is forgotten.

I suspect that the essence of good teaching lies in this baring of one's Being and humanity, where content material and teaching methods are enmeshed with a person's experience of life. For good teachers the content and method *are* the person, and they illuminate and enlarge the world and its possibilities in each of their students. Like the work of art, they cause the student to ask: 'what is my self-understanding, what do I know, how has my understanding been enriched, what new world have I seen through this subject matter, what have I learned about the nature of teaching, what have I learned about the teacher as a human being, what have I learned about my own being?' And the way the student answers these questions creates, enriches and discloses the student as a person. Like a work of art, the spirit of the teacher abides.

When we speak of learning, therefore, we are talking about a complex, inseparable, holistic 'happening'. Learning is a general kind of human experience, which has much in common with the way Gadamer (1975: 190) speaks of reading a work as 'an event, a happening that takes place in time, and the meaning of the work for us is a product of the integration of our own present horizon and that of the work'.

What of the role of the staff developer in this? It does not mean that technical, 'nuts and bolts' advice and prescription has no place. It *does* mean that the place of such advice is limited, and that the developer can play a larger role in his or her relationships with staff. Gadamer outlines three ways of viewing one's relationships with others.

The first of these occurs when we see the other person as a means of achieving our own goals. The other person becomes an object, undifferentiated, another unit which needs to be 'developed' and receive instruction on what constitutes 'right thinking'. For example, people generally may not accept the worth of student evaluations of teaching, they dismiss learning contracts, they chose not to use participative methods in their classes. Problems are seen as universal and the application of an 'objective' method is called for. Gadamer terms this an 'I–thou' relationship.

The second kind of relationship recognizes the other person as a subjective, thinking, self-reflective human being, and not simply a single unit of an undifferentiated mass. The trouble is that this person is not 'right thinking' on a particular issue (student evaluations, learning contracts, participative methods, etc.). The kind of interpretation used is: 'I know what is best for this person and although they do not recognize this themself, in time they will come to see the truth'. Tellingly, in commenting on this kind of relationship, Gadamer (1975: 323) claims that: 'We are familiar with this from the educative relationship, an authoritative form of welfare work'. The relationship is one of 'I–you', where the 'I' fails to acknowledge his or her prejudices and fails to appreciate that he or she is no more than a participant in a conversational (dialogical) process.

The third kind of relationship is one of 'authentic openness' to the other (both Heidegger and Gadamer use the word 'authenticity'). The attitude it conveys has profound importance for educational and staff developers. It is an attitude of listening, of letting the other speak, of seeking understanding and having a willingness to be modified by the other. It is not a relationship of mastery or control. We are revisiting themes raised earlier in the chapter and best illustrated in Gadamer's own words:

> The hermeneutical consciousness has its fulfilment, not in its methodological sureness of itself, but in the same readiness for experience

that distinguishes the experienced man by comparison with the man captivated by dogma.

(Gadamer 1975: 325)

Without this kind of openness to one another there is no genuine human relationship.

(Gadamer 1975: 324)

'Authenticity' in terms of openness to the other is a fundamental requirement for educational and staff development. It does not involve 'neutrality' towards a particular issue or the extinction of one's self. The important thing is to be aware and to become further aware of one's own prejudice and bias as the staff development conversation unfolds. Examples cited above involve student evaluations of teaching, learning contracts, active participation by students in classes – and to these we could add very many more attitudes and practices which have come to be regarded as 'good', almost by definition. But the staff developer's task is to identify his or her prejudices and to hold these open to query as the staff development conversation ensues.

Of course, not all of the developer's prejudices will be recognized, nor will each one be unhelpful. Prejudice is inevitable, and Gadamer explains at some length how 'prejudice against prejudice' is unwarranted. As he says, 'the present is seen and understood only through the intention, ways of seeing, and preconceptions bequeathed from the past' (Gadamer 1975: 176). We are immersed in the past and it permeates every act of understanding. Language is the main carrier of tradition, and, to use Heidegger's phrase, it is the house of being. Language, history and being are interfused – there is no possibility of standing outside language and history to objectively survey and report on the world.

But this is not the last word. Our historical, social, cultural, political or gender experience situates but does not isolate us. Gadamer (1975: 269) shows how our 'situation' leads to a horizon of sight:

Every finite present has its limitations. We define the concept of 'situation' by saying that it represents a standpoint that limits the possibility of vision. Hence an essential part of the concept of situation is the concept of 'horizon.' The horizon is the range of vision that includes everything that can be seen from a particular vantage point.

A horizon may be limited, therefore, but it is also open and subject to change as the observer moves position. Such movement is inevitable as time (history) changes our view of the present into a view of the past. The difference experienced by individuals, societies or even scientific paradigms also ensures a variety of standpoints from which to view and interpret the world: a difference of horizon. The idea that cultures, historical periods or gender positions are essentially closed is itself an abstraction, and one which Gadamer would reject. As we seek to understand others, there is always the possibility of a 'fusion of horizons' which enlarges and enriches our own horizon. We do not 'bracket' our own understanding to make this possible. We cannot put on hold or escape our own 'prejudices'. But we *can* risk and test them. As we do this we are, in the true spirit of hermeneutics, coming to a fuller understanding of ourselves and to a greater self-knowledge.

The way to such understanding is through dialogue and conversation, in which there is

> not only the common bond and the genuine novelty that a turn in a conversation may take but the mutuality, the respect required, the genuine seeking to listen to and understand what the other is say-ing, the openness to risk and test our own opinions through such an encounter.
>
> (Bernstein 1983: 162)

Freedom to learn a way of being

An unstated theme running through this chapter, and undoubtedly an uncomfortable one for some, has been a view of the educational and staff developer as counsellor and therapist. It is interesting, then, to find some support for this position from humanistic educators writing from their own experience and with little knowledge of the Hermes tradition. In the next two sections I will take a highly selective look at the notion of understand-ing outside of its traditional hermeneutical setting and as it has emerged in educational practice.

The title of this subsection is a conjunction of titles by the person who has perhaps done most to popularize humanistic psychology and education and to reassert therapy as a normal part of communication. That person is Carl Rogers.

It is unlikely that Rogers was very well acquainted with hermeneutics. In 1985, he mentioned Bleicher's *Contemporary Hermeneutics* (1980), and in giving an outline of this work shows his understanding of hermeneutics to be fairly rudimentary (Rogers 1985; reprinted in Rogers 1989a). He died just two years later. It is remarkable, therefore, that Rogers appears to have discovered for himself many of the paths travelled by hermeneuticians before him.

Having started out to write only for therapists, Rogers was astounded that his books brought a much wider response from many other parts of the 'people'-orientated professions. It brought him to see that 'all my writing ... contains the realization that what is true in a relationship between therapist and client may well be true for a marriage, a family, a school, an administration, a relationship between cultures or countries' (Rogers 1980: viii). Rogers was one of a very few to recognize explicitly the therapeutic aspect of communication. For those of us who are staff developers, this is a part of our work which we are perhaps reluctant to accept, but which needs our attention.

To read Rogers is to be constantly reminded of basic hermeneutical insights, which he caringly interweaves with his experiences. Perhaps his greatest strength is that he writes from his own life and what he has learned. For example, *A Way of Being* (1980) opens with a description of an invited address on the subject of 'Communication' which he had been asked to give at Caltech. He immediately contextualizes the event and paints himself into the scene. He opens the address by explaining that 'I would like, rather than talking *about* communication, to *communicate* with you at a feeling level' (Rogers 1980: 6). He explains that this is not an easy thing to do, that before the address he had doubts about being able to do it at all, but that he received support from a number of sources, including his wife. Within the first couple of minutes of the address, Rogers is communicating *himself* and thus his message. Reduced to printed words on a page, and 30 years later, the authenticity, openness and honesty of the communication shine through.

In the address he says how in talking with others he has come 'to feel expanded, larger, enriched', whereas at other times he has felt 'diminished or stopped or even reversed' (Rogers 1980: 7). The elements contributing to successful communication (or understanding) are again familiar. There is 'enjoyment when I really *hear* someone' which both 'puts me in touch' with the person and 'enriches my life' (Rogers 1980: 7–8). Really hearing means

> that I hear the words, the thoughts, the feeling tones, the personal meaning, even the meaning that is below the conscious intent of the speaker. Sometimes too, in a message which superficially is not very important, I hear a deep human cry that lies buried and unknown far below the surface of the person.
>
> (Rogers 1980: 8)

Rogers talks of the relief a person can have when someone 'really hears' them. It is as if they have been a prisoner in a cell, tapping out a message which has received no response, until one day the prisoner hears the taps which signal a response. By being heard, the person is released from their loneliness; they have 'become a human being again'.

Rogers is talking about the (emotional and cognitive) completeness of human understanding, the importance of empathy and authenticity, but he is going beyond this to the notion that such understanding is the basic condition of human being. As we have seen, this sits comfortably with Heidegger and Gadamer.

The people Rogers identifies as having listened to him and to have heard him have done so

> without judging me, diagnosing me, appraising me, evaluating me . . . when someone really hears you without passing judgement on you, without trying to take responsibility for you, without trying to mould you, it feels damn good!
>
> (Rogers 1980: 12)

Rogers admits that when he tries to 'really hear' another person himself, he often tries to twist the message into what he wants to hear, makes the problem into what he wants it to be, makes the person into what he wants that person to be. Again, this has a familiar ring to it; the dilemma for the staff developer is in attempting to remain non-judgemental within the relationship while at the same time having (often strong) convictions concerning what constitutes good teaching practice and the promotion of 'good' or 'appropriate' learning.

Roger's next observation is to point out what big risks are involved when we try to express something deeply from within, from our own private world. We can be humiliated when others do not pick up on our intentions. I have seen a number of examples of this when lecturers have laid themselves open to students, only to be met with condescension, apathy or, worse, derision. I have heard lecturers talk about such experiences and vow never to expose themselves to such risk again. That is a great pity for it is often in the highly personal account of a lecturer's experience that students gain more than 'cognition'; they share the lecturer's horizon of experience, gain entry to the lecturer's world and are exposed to the kind of 'understanding' that has been elaborated throughout this chapter.

There are shades here of what Gadamer calls 'creative negativity'. For each of us, experience is constantly to be acquired and no one can spare us from it. It is often painful and unpleasant as our expectations are challenged and defeated: thus the 'negativity'. The experienced teacher (or any experienced person) knows the limits of anticipation and the insecurity of plans but this makes them open for new experience, rather than dogmatic and rigid. This is the 'creative' side of a negative experience. Folk wisdom tells us that 'we learn from our mistakes', and 'nothing ventured, nothing gained'.

Perhaps the main lesson to be learned from lecturers having their attempts to engage students at a personal level spurned, is that the unusualness of the attempt says much about the normal nature of the relationship between lecturer and students. If the lecturer were routinely engaging in a direct, personal encounter with students, then such events might be less traumatic and the lecturer would also feel comfortable in responding to the students' reaction. The realization of vulnerability on either side of a relationship is an important element in opening up the relationship. Exactly the same thing applies, of course, to the relationship between staff developer and lecturer.

For Rogers (1980: 26), then, the major elements of developing understanding (what he calls communication) are:

A sensitive ability to hear, a deep satisfaction in being heard; an ability to be more real, which in turn brings forth more realness for others; and consequently a greater freedom to give and receive love – these, in my experience, are the elements that make interpersonal communication enriching and enhancing.

If Rogers is right, then relationships such as those between developer and lecturer, or lecturer and students, must be seen in a very different light to the 'neutral', 'professional', 'instrumental' and 'technical' values discussed in Chapter 2 above. Rogers went on to elaborate his view of learning and the facilitation of learning in *Freedom to Learn* (1969), and that book is still a classic exposition of humanistic education. It has certainly had an influence on writers whose books are used routinely for practical educational development activities (such as Knowles 1980; Heron 1989) and is often cited in the adult education and 'self-directed' literature (see, for example, Boud *et al.* 1985; Boud and Griffin 1987; Candy 1991; Hammond and Collins 1991).

Rogers (1969: 164–5) also outlined what he saw as the teacher's role in the facilitation of learning, which I will quote directly.

1. The facilitator has much to do with setting the initial mood or climate of the group or class experience. If his own basic philosophy is one of trust in the group and in the individuals who compose the group, then this point of view will be communicated in many subtle ways.
2. The facilitator helps to elicit and clarify the purposes of the individuals in the class as well as the more general purposes of the group . . . He can permit a diversity of purposes to exist, contradictory and complementary, in relationship to each other.
3. He relies upon the desire of each student to implement those purposes which have meaning for him, as the motivational force behind significant learning. Even if the desire of the student is to be guided and led by someone else, the facilitator can accept such a need and motive and can either serve as a guide . . . or can provide some other means . . .
4. He endeavours to organize and make easily available the widest possible range of resources for learning.

5. He regards himself as a flexible resource to be utilized by the group.
6. In responding to expressions in the classroom group, he accepts both the intellectual content and the emotionalized attitudes ... he accepts rationalizations and intellectualizing, as well as deep and real personal feelings.
7. As the acceptant classroom climate becomes established, the facilitator is able increasingly to become a participant learner, a member of the group, expressing his views as those of one individual only.
8. He takes the initiative in sharing himself with the group – his feelings as well as his thoughts – in ways which do not demand [or] impose but represent simply a personal sharing which students may take or leave.
9. Throughout the classroom experience, he remains alert to the expressions indicative of deep or strong feelings.
10. In his functioning as a facilitator of learning, the leader endeavours to recognize and accept his own limitations.

Propositions such as these are now quite commonplace in practically orientated books concerning teaching, learning and process facilitation in higher education. I believe it is important for staff developers to understand the background to the practical advice offered. In short, the humanistic psychology and education from which it comes is best seen as a modern, practical and popular formulation of the hermeneutical tradition of understanding and interpretation.

The messages for staff and educational developers follow similar lines to those we have encountered previously. According to this perspective, the development of a person's educational practice is a humanist project emphasizing each individual's autonomy, personal responsibility, personal needs, personal and emotional commitment. There is a belief that each human being has a propensity for personal and self-directed growth and development. The place of the staff developer (as of the teacher) is to facilitate the process, and Rogers has something to say on appropriate techniques. His approach is non-directive; most commonly the counsellor 'recognizes in some way the feeling or attitude which the client has just expressed' and 'interprets or recognizes feelings or attitudes expressed by general demeanor, specific behaviour, or earlier statements'. In contrast to this, a directive counsellor 'asks highly specific questions, delimiting answers to yes, no, or specific information [and] explains, discusses, or gives information related to the problem or treatment' (Rogers 1942; reprinted in Rogers 1989b: 63). In adopting a non-directional approach, the staff developer, sharing in a common humanity, is cast as therapist.

The reflective practitioner

It is interesting that the whole of Carl Rogers's self-confessed 'credo' is quoted by the person most associated with the notion of reflective practice – Donald Schön – in his book *Educating the Reflective Practitioner* (1990). His original book, *The Reflective Practitioner* (1983), is in essence an interpretation of what professional practice looks like if viewed from a hermeneutical as opposed to a positivistic stance. He believes that 'reflective practice' should replace the 'technical-rational' tradition of professional practice. The technical-rational model accords with a view of the world which we saw in the previous chapter was born of the Enlightenment, the search for positive knowledge and the adoption of an instrumental value system. From this perspective, professional practice rests upon an underlying discipline or basic science producing general theory and knowledge which the professional practitioner then *applies* to individual daily problems. Basic disciplinary knowledge or science is thus the starting point. Knowing directs doing, and those who know are the experts. Medical doctors, for example, learn basic science disciplines (anatomy, physiology, etc.) and then apply this knowledge in their professional practice. They are experts because of their scientific knowledge. Again, we saw in Chapter 2 how staff development may also be viewed in this way, with the staff developer as 'learning theory' or 'teaching' expert, applying this privileged knowledge to upgrade the ability of neophytes through technical programmes of skills development.

By comparison, reflective practice is more tenuous and unsure of its basic knowledge claims and, again, more convinced of the importance of *experience*. The reflective practitioner finds it impossible to extricate knowing and doing. Schön (1983: 49) sums it up as follows:

> When we go about the spontaneous, intuitive performance of the actions of everyday life, we show ourselves to be knowledgeable in a special way. Often we cannot say what it is that we know. When we try to describe it we find ourselves at a loss, or we produce descriptions that are obviously inappropriate. Our knowledge is ordinarily tacit, implicit in our patterns of action and in our feel for the stuff with which we are dealing. It seems right to say that our knowing is *in* our action.

For Schön there are important consequences which flow from the differing stances taken by the 'expert' and the 'reflective practitioner.' These are summarized in Table 1.

Once more we find common ground with insights from the hermeneutical tradition, as Schön speaks of uncertainty, learning from each other, seeking out connections to the client's thoughts and feelings, freedom, and real

Table 1   Comparative stances of the expert and reflective practitioner.

Expert	Reflective practitioner
I am presumed to know, and must claim to do so, regardless of my own uncertainty.	I am presumed to know, but I am not the only one in the situation to have relevant and important knowledge. My uncertainties may be a source of learning for me and for them.
Keep my distance from the client, and hold on to the expert's role. Give the client a sense of my expertise, but convey a feeling of warmth and sympathy as a 'sweetener'.	Seek out connections to the client's thoughts and feelings. Allow his respect for my knowledge to emerge from his discovery of it in the situation.
Look for deference and status in the client's response to my professional persona.	Look for the sense of freedom and of real connection to the client, as a consequence of no longer needing to maintain a professional façade.

Source: Schön (1983: 300)

connection to the client. Schön (1983) also refers back to his earlier work with Chris Argyris (Argyris and Schön 1974) in which two models of values and behaviour are described. Model I includes: dominating the definition and process of achieving the task; trying to win; avoiding anger and resentment; being rational, cool and persuasive; pointing out or offering external rewards or punishments. By contrast, Model II behaviour encourages: the creation of conditions for free and informed choice; awareness of the values at stake; awareness of the limitations of one's own capacities; each person having internal commitment to decisions; and commitment being based on intrinsic satisfaction rather than external reward or punishment. Again, we appear to be replaying scenes from Gadamer's 'I–thou', 'I–you' and the 'authentic openness' required for relationships. But as with Rogers, it appears that Schön has little knowledge of the hermeneutical tradition and he cites no hermeneutical source or figure.

Many staff and educational developers would claim that they attempt to follow Schön's precepts of reflective practice. Many use books giving practical advice on the facilitation of learning, building group dynamics, fostering good communication between lecturer and student, much of which originated in the writings of Carl Rogers. I would claim both to be branches on the trunk of hermeneutics. I note my frustration that the full tradition of hermeneutics remains unacknowledged and that hermeneutical insight seems to find only very limited recognition in educational and staff development. Even the partial renditions seem prone to disappearance, and partial resurrection at a later date. There still remains a disturbing lack of understanding of the main thrust of hermeneutical thought.

Conclusion

In this chapter I have considered elements of a view of educational and staff development from the perspective offered by hermeneutics. Based in 'life philosophy' and the acknowledgment of our common humanity, these perspectives include the importance of empathy and the 'understanding' of others, with all the richness this understanding can embrace. It places human relationships centre-stage. It also includes the ontological insight of our being-in-the-world before all else and our consciousness of our own being. It denies developmental notions of human beings as incomplete. Each person is taken seriously as an entity, and universal programmes and prescriptions are impossible. Nor are there method-driven ways of pursuing development. Instead, development is seen as an open-ended process which can effect and change both parties:

> truth has the nature of a process. It has to do with the 'modes of being' that shape human existence. Hence, truth appears within temporality, action, and relationality. Truth is no longer taken to be synonymous with a theory of knowledge but addresses modes of human existence.
> (DiCenso 1990: 146–7)

A staff development episode may come out differently depending on the individual, the situation in time and space, and the nature of the relationship. Prescriptive ethics (such as student autonomy, student-centred or self-directed learning) are finite and can be intolerant and repressive if not subjected to the interpretative structures of the individuals involved. One journeys into these areas anew each time, working the circles of interpretation and understanding, rather than haranguing others to convert to the truth. Apart from the main trunk of hermeneutics, some of these elements have also found their ways into the educational development discourse, particularly in the writings of Carl Rogers and Donald Schön.

But the view of staff development afforded by hermeneutics is not complete, and has its own attendant problems. A major problem concerns power. With a view of staff development as dialogue, discussion or conversation, the unequal distribution of power between the conversationalists is obviously of concern. The staff developer and lecturer, the lecturer and students, are not equally empowered or equally invited into the discourse of learning, teaching and staff development. Also, unequal power distributions follow societal norms with regard to such things as class, gender and ethnicity. Traditional hermeneutics and humanistic psychology and education have much to say concerning our 'common humanity' and our wishes for personal fulfilment, but less to say about our social and cultural identity and the unequal ways in which this affects our ability to speak openly with each other. This is the domain of critical hermeneutics or critical theory, and is the basis for action research. It is to the view of staff development afforded by this perspective that we turn next.

Notes

1. The Greek verb *hermeneuein* is translated as 'to interpret' and the noun *hermeneia* as 'interpretation'. These may have derived from 'Hermes', or vice versa.
2. The concept of *Verstehen* had been outlined a little earlier by the German historian, J. G. Droysen. It was taken up by Dilthey and later hermeneuticians and became crucial to the development of *Geisteswissenschaften*.
3. Husserl's phenomenology is discussed in the context of phenomenography in Chapter 5.

4

To Critically Go: Staff Development for a Better World

The philosophers have only *interpreted* the world in different ways; the point is to change it.

(Quoted from Marx: Theses on Feuerbach, 1845)

Introduction

In the two preceding chapters of this book, quite different conceptions for the consideration and interpretation of education and staff development have been outlined. In terms of a theory of knowledge, the position which advocated positive knowledge or positivism as the foundation for practice has been criticized as lacking insight into basic human understanding. On the other hand, hermeneutics places humanity and understanding in the foreground. It is by gaining 'understanding' of our shared humanity and of the position, concerns, thoughts and feelings of others, that we might help them learn and develop. But what are the consequences of unequal power in the conversation between people as they strive for mutual understanding, and what if we learn how another person sees the world, gain a deep and empathic understanding of that person's position, and still consider it to be wrong? In other words, is there a reliable compass by which we may set direction and chart our educational or staff development activities? In this chapter we consider claims that a 'critical theory' of society can inform our direction and that progress in this preferred direction may be made through action research.

Apart from phenomenography, action research is perhaps the most influential and almost certainly the fastest-growing orientation towards staff development at the present time. Not surprisingly, the focus of this orientation is upon *action*. It is concerned with change, but change in a particular direction. It is argued that behind action research lies a philosophical tradition which legitimizes and spurs change for the betterment of humanity. Staff development is concerned with change, too. If action research really can help us to decide what is better, then perhaps it can help us to resolve some of the suspicions and doubts which were raised in

Chapter 2. There we saw how notions of development, evolution and progress come complete with a baggage and set of problems of their own. If action research can inform us about what is meant by 'better', then this would represent a major step forward. And if better staff development means increasing the participation of or giving a 'voice' to both teachers and students; collaboration on an equal footing; open-ended and progressive enquiry; the emancipation of those involved – then we begin to see why for staff developers the prospect of action research holds much hope.

The chapter begins by looking at the origins of the social and critical theory which has become associated with action research and then traces some of the consequences of this view of the world. This is followed by a critique of critical theory and action research in which the case is put that these positions are significantly flawed in their ability to clearly direct our efforts.

From Hegel to Marx

We have already seen how Plato's theory of forms took perceived reality to be but an imperfect reflection of timeless and absolute truths. The French and English development of empiricism, science and an Enlightenment spirit of universal human progress suggested that these truths were open to discovery. Alternatively, as part of the German inclination towards metaphysics and disclosure, G. W. F. Hegel developed a universal method which he called the *dialectic*.[1] Essentially this involved the notion that a particular point of view (thesis) and its counter-argument (antithesis) could both contain elements of truth. The dialectical method comprises bringing the truth from each side together in a new formulation (synthesis). He also believed that ultimate truth and reason were not given to individuals but was vested in social groups. The primary social group of Hegel's time was the nation, and it was in the unfolding of social forces through national rivalry that Hegel saw the development of historical necessity. The Hegelian innovations of the (modern) dialectic and of the social group as arbiter of reason produced the seed-bed for Marxism, critical theory and, ultimately, the emancipatory form of action research.

Marx replaced Hegel's insistence upon the nation as the unit of struggle in producing social history with a new focus upon class. History could be explained in terms of a class struggle, with each class representing a particular economic interest and relationship towards power. For both Hegel and Marx there was an inevitability in the way that history would unfold, and this inevitability comprised both a causal explanation of what *would* happen and a moral justification of what *should* happen. The dialectic of Marx took the struggle of classes as the means by which social progress and higher moral values would be realized. Marx saw power as the final arbiter of progress and was sceptical of ameliorative measures or political progress through negotiation and accommodation. With hindsight, he offered little assurance that power in the hands of a new class interest (the proletariat) would be used in a less authoritarian or wiser way than it had in the hands of any previous ruling group.

Both Hegel and Marx saw history as a rational unfolding of progress towards a predetermined and higher goal. As products of their age, they were both essentially developmentalists. However, Hegel's vision was of Germany as the spiritual leader in the progress of European nations, whereas Marx's vision was of the proletariat as the leader of emancipation and social justice for all. Both views have similar consequences for the action of individuals, in that the appeal was 'to loyalty rather than to self-interest, to duties rather than to rights, and it offered no reward except the hope that one's private life would gain meaning through service to a cause greater than oneself' (Sabine 1963: 759).

There is a challenge to individualism in the vesting of legitimacy and moral aspiration in the group, and this is a constant theme in the development of this branch of social theory. It is important to note, however, that the 'necessity' or 'inevitability' which both Hegel and Marx saw in history should be viewed as a call to action and a moral obligation. It is individual action which spurs change, and without action progressive movements cannot eventuate. It is the duty of each one of us to join the march of progress towards a historically inevitable future, and in so doing to play our part in purging 'irrationalism' along the way.

Critical theory

Karl Marx died in 1883. The broad-based proletarian revolution he predicted for Germany and elsewhere in western Europe had not happened, and the fundamentally flawed economic system of capitalism was proving resilient to the inevitable march of history. On the other hand, in Russia, an agrarian and semi-feudal society that had barely experienced a bourgeois (democratic) revolution, Lenin led a successful revolt spearheaded by a tiny Communist Party. Faced with changed circumstances, German intellectuals in 1923 founded the Institute for Social Research in Frankfurt which

> became the first formally unaffiliated Marxist-oriented institute in Europe ... its members attempted to revise both the Marxian critique of capitalism and the theory of revolution in order to confront those new social and political conditions which had evolved since Marx's death. In the process a 'critical theory' of society emerged to deal with

those aspects of social reality which Marx and his orthodox followers neglected or downplayed.

(Bronner and Kellner 1989: 1)

The 'Frankfurt School' of 'critical theory' has been one of the major instruments through which social reform, social theory and the message of socialism have been carried from their nineteenth-century Marxian roots into current debate. This is all the more surprising as the term 'critical theory' was first used in 1937 when most of the Institute's members had already fled Hitler's Germany for the United States.[2] 'Critical theory' was in fact a euphemism made necessary by the abhorrence with which any suggestion of Marxism was greeted in the United States. The first generation of critical theorists included Max Horkheimer, Theodor Adorno, Leo Lowenthal, Herbert Marcuse and Erich Fromm.[3] Jürgen Habermas is the major figure of the second generation, and it is Habermas's work which will be outlined in a little detail.

The early critical theorists were worried by the way science and its positivist view of the world had become accepted as the bench-mark for any kind of thinking or acting and especially for thinking about society. Rationality had become defined according to science. Science was seen as being able to produce 'the facts' upon which social action could be based, but the values underlying these facts and the direction in which society *should* be travelling were outside its scope. Normative and critical questions of where society was going and why, had been replaced by technical and instrumental questions. Science tended to consider whether a particular course of action was more efficient or effective than another, taking for granted that the end point was desirable. The task which Habermas took up was to show that 'scientific' or instrumental knowledge is but one way of thinking, and one which is not particularly valuable in giving direction to social action (including consideration of what should happen in education).

His approach was to ask the basic question of why knowledge was produced at all. The answer he came up with was that knowledge is always produced for a purpose: it is produced because people want to know something. Knowledge is not produced from the 'disinterested' enquiry of minds, it is produced because of the basic needs or interests of humankind. These interests, (which he refers to as 'knowledge-constitutive interests') he took as given or *a priori*. According to Habermas there are three of them: the technical interest; the practical interest; and the emancipatory interest. The technical interest of people is to acquire technical control over the natural world and is the domain of science and technology. The practical interest (somewhat curiously named) refers to the interest of people in understanding each other and interpreting social practices. It is the domain of hermeneutics and the tradition of *verstehen* elaborated in the previous chapter.

According to Habermas, the problem with this standpoint is that there exist objective social, political, economic – *power* – relationships which distort people's subjective appreciation of the world. Coming to an hermeneutical understanding of a person or group is one thing, but that person or group may articulate a view of the world which is false or against their own 'true' interests. Only if they have autonomy and freedom can they give a 'true' account of their own interests. Also, only if there are equal, fair and democratic procedures in place will their voice be heard. For these reasons, the effective communication assumed by the hermeneutical tradition can only occur when appropriate and supportive social conditions apply. To put such conditions in place, which in the long term is in everyone's interest, is the basic human interest of emancipation, or the emancipatory interest. It is for a critical social science to show people how they are oppressed, how their interests have become repressed or distorted, and what life will look like when they have confronted their oppressions, changed their conditions and moved towards a more rational society.

What is a more rational society? To answer this, Habermas turns to language and discourse. He claims that the point of speech is to communicate, to test counter-positions and to gain understanding. In an 'ideal speech situation' each person is equally empowered to speak, there is no coercion from outside the conversation or between the discussants, and it is the power of the argument rather than the power of a particular person which carries the day. The very point of language in making it possible for communication to take place, is underlain by the idea of the 'ideal speech situation', which in turn is the model for a rational society and, interestingly, for science, too. The ideal speech situation lies at the base of all communication, and the conditions which come closest to the ideal at this microcosmic level provide the blueprint for a just and rational society. Again, the blueprint is of an open community with each person able to participate fully, where the community is convinced by the force of the argument rather than by the power of the presenter. The same conditions apply similarly for scientific enquirers participating in an open, healthy and robust scientific community.[4]

Critical theory in education

It is hardly surprising that the attempt to provide such a foundational explanation and direction for communication, science and society has also attracted the attention of educators. If Habermas is right, then there are implications for our understanding of the place and process of education not only with respect to knowledge and enquiry but also in terms of social justice. It also follows that there are implications for the philosophy and practice of staff development.

Mezirow (1981) was one of the first to bring the ideas of Habermas into the mainstream of educational thinking. His paper opens with the words: 'This article presents the beginnings of a critical theory of adult learning and education' (Mezirow 1981: 3). Critical theory is directly embraced, and, according to Mezirow, the three 'knowledge-constitutive interests' have direct corollaries in learning: 'as each domain has its own learning goal (viz., learning for task-related competence, learning for interpersonal understanding and learning for perspective transformation), learning needs, approaches for facilitating learning, methods of research and program evaluation are implied or explicit' (Mezirow 1981: 16).

Mezirow elaborates the three knowledge domains in terms of this relationship to learning. The 'technical' is task-orientated and can be associated with behavioural objectives, competency-based learning, skills training, criterion-referenced testing and empirical research and evaluation. The 'practical' domain emphasizes empathy with others which can be developed as teachers encourage their students to 'take the role of others ... develop empathy and ... confidence and competence in such aspects of human relations as resolving conflict, participating in discussion and dialogue, participating and leading in learning groups, listening, expressing oneself, asking questions, philosophizing' (Mezirow 1981: 18).

But it is in the third domain that Mezirow has most to say. Here, Habermas's 'emancipatory' reason for knowledge becomes 'learning for perspective transformation' and is linked to other educational ideas. For example, 'meta-learning', the process by which learners become aware and take control of their learning, is said to be common in many learning situations, including the technical and practical. It is a necessary but not a sufficient condition for perspective transformation. To undertake learning which is perspective-transforming (or emancipatory) one must be aware not only of one's own thinking but also 'the cultural assumptions governing the rules, roles, conventions and social expectations which dictate the way we see, think, feel and act' (Mezirow 1981: 13). To achieve this appreciation we need 'critical awareness' or 'critical consciousness': we need to be aware of our own awareness and capable of critiquing it.

How is this to be accomplished? Here Mezirow turns to Paulo Freire (1970), the radical Brazilian educator, who suggests the need to start from the problems and perspectives of the learner and from these to develop materials which pose dilemmas. Socratic dialogue may then be used in small-group settings where experiences are shared, group solidarity and support developed, and a new perspective achieved. When people come together with a common problem, the early phase of pointing out the problem may be unnecessary and support groups, approximating the 'ideal speech situation', can take off from the beginning. Whatever the starting point, the main objective is clear and important:

bringing psycho-cultural assumptions into critical consciousness to help a person understand how he or she has come into possession of conceptual categories, rules, tactics and criteria for judging . . . perception, thought and behavior involves perhaps the most significant kind of learning. It increases a crucial sense of agency over ourselves and our lives.

(Mezirow 1981: 20)

So the knowledge which education may give us by this process of self-reflection in the context of ideology critique represents the most significant kind of learning we can achieve. What is more, it is the imperative of educators to ensure that such learning takes place.

Learners *must* . . . be led to an understanding of the reasons imbedded in these internalized cultural myths and concomitant feelings which account for . . . the way they see themselves and their relations . . . learners *must* be given access to alternative meaning perspectives for interpreting this reality so that critique of these psycho-cultural assumptions is possible.

(Mezirow 1981: 18; emphasis added)

We see here shades of the Marxist tendency to evangelize which results from an exaggerated confidence in a particular opinion. People must be saved, even from themselves. They may not want to face the truth of their exploitation and repression, they may even claim that they are not repressed, but they only say this because they cannot see through the ideology which surrounds and defines them. Just as it was the responsibility of the revolutionary class to ensure that in such conditions of 'false consciousness' people are saved from themselves, so, too, it is the responsibility of educators to ensure that people see the world 'properly'. And just as developmentalists always claim the 'right' interpretation of people's problems, so, too, critical theorists are the ones looking through the correct pair of glasses.

Staff development from the stance of critical theory would ideally expect staff members spontaneously to come together as they realize that their common interests promote a common purpose and solidarity and that amelioration of the conditions which oppress them lies in their own hands. For example, it might be that the failure of students to take more than an instrumental or credentialing view of learning may be traced neither to the individual student, nor to the type of instruction, nor to the departmental context. Instead, a wider critique of the nature of society in terms of its institutionalization of competitive relationships could be mounted. Education might be viewed as but a part of the socialization of the next generation's élite, and this would help explain the difficulty 'non-traditional' groups have in gaining entrance. Education acts as the gatekeeper to privilege and as the supplier of labour to capitalist enterprise.[5] The pathologies of society are also manifested in such diverse areas as sexism and racism in the curriculum, and the rationalist and managerialist orientation of the modern higher education institution. Such phenomena are to be resisted, and it is important to recognize that such resistance is played out in the curriculum. However, the confrontation of these issues in the curriculum is only one part of the story, as we should also be 'good citizens' by confronting them at the wider societal level. It is our duty to participate in 'making a better world'.

The staff developer's role in all of this is reminiscent of Lenin's view of the communist party. It is a role of leadership and facilitation – staff developers are in the vanguard of the movement towards better educational methods; they mirror the values of a better institution and ultimately a better society. Staff developers may be catalysts of progressive transformation and of progressive pedagogy. The early socialists found that there was little use in waiting for a spontaneous uprising: it is the duty of those in the vanguard to lead the way. Even though they represent a small number of those involved, they are the ones with a clear view of the future. They must not shirk their responsibility. Thus the staff developer leads and facilitates 'action' projects to improve learning, guided by the precepts of group-based activity, equality, democracy and emancipation. We are talking here of the role of the staff developer in 'action research' projects.

Action research

The term 'action research' was coined by Kurt Lewin (see, for example, Lewin 1946), an American sociologist working on a range of community projects concerning integration and social justice in areas such as housing and employment.[6] Lewin's work in underprivileged communities was taken up by Stephen Corey (see, for example, Corey 1949) who was concerned that research into teaching should have a practical effect on classroom practices. His collaborative research projects for teachers were further developed by John Elliot (see, for example, Elliot and Adelman 1973) in the Ford teaching project and generalized in later writings (for example, Elliot 1978). Essentially practical endeavours such as these later become explicitly linked to critical theory and in particular the work of Habermas in Carr and Kemmis's important book, *Becoming Critical: Education, Knowledge and Action Research* (1986).

The method of action research also became somewhat codified into the moments of planning, acting, observing and reflecting. Having completed one such cycle, action researchers may then spiral into a further cycle, or into offshoot spirals (see McNiff 1988). What has become perhaps the standard definition of action research is given by Kemmis and McTaggart (1988a: 5–6):

Action research is a form of *collective* self-reflective enquiry undertaken by participants in social situations in order to improve the rationality and justice of their own social or educational practices, as well as their understanding of these practices and the situations in which these practices are carried out ... The approach is only action research when it is *collaborative*, though it is important to realise that the action research of the group is achieved through the *critically examined action* of individual group members.

We see here the collective (group) emphasis which reaches back to Hegel and Marx. Although there is an Enlightenment-like assurance that 'rationality and justice' can be improved, this is, of course, less a natural process of development and evolution than a moral imperative and obligation to become involved.

So how should staff developers be involved in action research projects? In theory, emancipatory action research follows from the spontaneous coming together of people with a common problem. It is unlikely in this case that the staff developer will be involved at all. Being largely outside the context, the staff developer may not have the same motivation and view of the problem as those more intimately concerned. In fact, it is far more likely that staff developers either will be called in for 'expert' advice on how to tackle a particular issue, or may themselves attempt to interest people and initiate projects (the catalytic role). The question of 'equality' then becomes interesting as the staff developer brings to the problem an expertise which the originators cannot provide themselves. Often the staff developer has greater general experience of pedagogy and a far better sense of the epistemology and methodology of educational research projects. The staff developer will be able to interpret a project more generally than other participants, to explain where it fits, point to useful literature and use previous experience to guide the development of the project. Inevitably the staff developer may become a central and crucial element in the project and take an active role in suggesting future directions, spin-offs or similar projects in different contexts. In short, the staff developer may find it hard to play the part of 'just another member' of a project team.

Should this cause us concern? I would argue that it is a point of which staff developers need to be acutely aware. In a 'pure' view of action research the inequality generated by the staff developer's expertise and different stance must certainly be construed as a cause of concern. However, it has always been a fiction that those with common interests start with common abilities or a common desire to contribute to a project group. 'Equality' as a starting point is a myth despite any number of declarations of intent and attempts to set ground rules. The ground rules are there *because* inequality exists in the opportunities for all to contribute to the group. It is important for group members to talk about their hopes and expectations concerning levels of participation and for the development of the group process to be monitored.

But it is a pity if participants enter the project with unrealistic expectations about working relationships. Often there is a binding together of an action research group as individuals come to discover their commonalities and find solace in each other in the face of the doubts and criticisms of those outside. Structural inequalities and human frailties may appear later as group members get to know each other better, find interests in the others to which they cannot relate, or aspects of them which they do not particularly like. Jealousy and friction are not easily banished, even for the common good.

Of course, much of this also applies equally to students learning in groups. The moral we may draw is that the adoption of a group-based approach, whether in learning or in professional development, does not constitute an assurance of virtue. Virtue needs to be demonstrated and earned, and it is worthwhile to urge some caution concerning an uncritical adoption of action research for the purpose of staff development.

Action research is presently gaining widespread acceptance in educational and staff development practice. Its claim to the moral high ground makes for difficulty if one chooses to criticize it, especially as some of its advocates display an evangelical faith. But as Gibson (1985: 60) points out in his engaging critique of Carr and Kemmis's *Becoming Critical* (after apologizing for the alarmingly long sentence):

> What's very worrying about this book is that it is intensely uncritical (i.e. it doesn't practice what it preaches); its prescriptions are likely to result in increased conformity, (i.e. it would produce its own rigid orthodoxy); it is naive about group processes; it prefers the group over the individual, and the in-group over the out-group; it is bedazzled by the notion of 'science'; it rejects objectivity, yet privileges its own view of reality; it is characterised by hubris (i.e. it lacks modesty in its claims and perceptions); it is highly contradictory (actually not a bad thing in the human condition but the book doesn't recognise its own contradictions); it has far too much respect for the authority of critical theory; it is an elitist text masquerading as an egalitarian one; it insufficiently acknowledges that action research at the three levels of the interpersonal (e.g. classroom), institutional (e.g. school or LEA), or structural (e.g. economic, political, ideological) involve different activities and levels of difficulty for would-be action researchers; and in its seeming preference for the institutional and structural levels, it is attempting to set action research off on a course very different from its present practice.

Gibson goes on to show how problematic and contestable can be many of the core notions of an action research based in critical theory. Both Hegel

and Marx were clear that the greater good would be served by the hege-
mony of one entity (the German state and the working class, respectively).
Action researchers can easily be led into denying their own partisan positions and claiming that their actions are for the good of all. The excesses
of communitarian politics are played out in miniature if groups become
carried away with building their own 'solidarity', manifestly or subtly encouraging their own conformity or, in short, becoming intolerant of alternative
views to their own. The idea that a 'rational' position may be reached when
all 'distortions' (to the correct view) have been eliminated is dangerous,
and, so, too, is the re-creation of the Marxist idea of 'false consciousness'.

The falsely conscious are those who believe and act against their own
'true' interests. An early example would be working-class supporters of
conservative politics, but in the educational sphere we could imagine students who do not want to work in groups, or lecturers who resist such
things as problem-based learning, or other examples of 'good practice'.
The trouble with false consciousness is that it is patronizing and gives one
group the power to ignore the views of another. This is not to say that the
views of any group must necessarily be viewed as equal. For example, it is
not necessary to believe that creationists or supporters of a flat earth theory
should be afforded equal time in the curriculum with geological explanation. But it does make incumbent upon a particular group, in rejecting the
views of others, that they explain their own partisan position and seek
legitimacy and continual reassurance in their use of power. After all, an
action research group may be accused of false consciousness and self-
delusion as readily as anyone else.

A similar point also applies to tensions between an individual and the
group. It may be claimed that just as groups can be deluded, so, too, might
an individual who does not submit to the critique of the collective. But
there is always the potential for tension between the aspirations and interests of individuals within a group. This applies in so-called 'communal' or
tribal societies just as it does in societies which emphasize individual rights.
The privileging of the group, solidarity and conformity over the individual
brings its own dangers.

Gibson (1985) points out that the vesting of power in a 'professional'
group is highly questionable. Much though teachers might wish the power
to determine what will be taught, how it will be taught and by whom, it is
not transparently clear that such an arrangement will serve the best interests of all. Those with interests in education (such as students, parents,
employers, professional bodies, government, etc.) are currently described
as 'stakeholders'. Teachers are certainly 'stakeholders' themselves, but
why should they as professionals, or a particular action research group of
professionals, lay claim to the only legitimate view of what is good for education? The same point can also be put to staff developers as they contemplate the foundation of national associations. To be an interest group is one

thing, to claim to be the only legitimate voice of educational and staff development is quite another.

In fact all the words which tend to appear on the side of the 'good and holy' in action research and critical theory are problematic and contestable. These include: emancipation, autonomy, democracy, consensus, rationality, solidarity, social justice and community. In the philosophy of education literature, articles abound testing and contesting what each of these words might mean and suggest for educational practice. As staff developers, we should maintain a healthy scepticism for the idealized turn taken in the coupling of action research and critical theory. As I have suggested elsewhere:

> We should not be too depressed . . . by the fact that critical theory may give us little more than the suggestion of a direction in which we wish to travel. Glimpses of ideals such as the good, the beautiful, the just, have perhaps always provided inspiration for the material practicality of and existential responsibility for, the decision making of everyday life.
>
> (Webb 1991: 41)

When it comes down to involvement in an action research project, the hermeneutical nature of the group process is often all important. Claims to ownership of rationality and a 'true' or 'undistorted' view of reality are likely to be unhelpful, to say the least.

Another interesting critique of action research as informed by critical theory is suggested by Fisher (1987). In particular, he examines Kemmis's use of the notion of 'dialectic' and points out the discrepancy between earlier Greek meanings associated with dialectic and later Hegelian and Marxist uses. Carr and Kemmis claim a unity of use from Aristotle to Hegel and Marx. However, there appear to be differences in what 'dialectics' means in differing historical contexts and with different usages. Carr and Kemmis adopt a modern usage seeing dialectics as a natural and social law (which is somewhat surprising given their following of the Habermasian distinction between the different knowledge-constitutive interests associated with the natural world and the human and social world). At the same time they try to use 'dialectic' as a way of combining the theory and practice of education under the Aristotelian notion of *praxis*, where each informs and develops the other. *Praxis* is itself informed by *phronesis*: the moral disposition to act truly and wisely. They consider that this arrangement is better for the theory and practice of education than the other Aristotelian categories of *episteme* (knowledge gained through contemplative or 'pure' philosophical thought) and *techne* (the kind of knowledge used in craft or trade and based on guiding rules, plans or images). *Praxis* based upon *phronesis* is then equated with the emancipatory interest of Habermas.

According to Fisher, the problem with this is that the (modern) view of dialectics as a law of nature and society is hard pressed to withstand the critique mounted from the philosophy of science. A view of dialectics which argues the unity of opposites is at odds with the principle of non-contradiction which is the corner-stone of formal logic. That is acceptable if one rejects such a notion of rationality itself (as much postmodern analysis would), but Carr and Kemmis lay claims to rationality not only in terms of science, but also of education as emancipatory science. Nor can dialectics be argued as a restatement of scientific method: at best there are some similarities between the two. Popper (1962; 1974) covered this ground in his critiques of dialectics as a 'scientific' method and the dangers it poses for an open society.

Let us return to the action research group (or community) pursuing its inquiries. How are differences of opinion or interpretation within the group to be resolved? How is it possible to argue a case against a dialectician who insists on a thing being both one thing and something else? How is the happy consensus (synthesis or emancipatory interest) necessarily arrived at: are there no grounds for clear and honest disagreement about what the synthesis or emancipatory course of action should be? And in such cases how is the 'right' course (the emancipatory interest) decided? Democracy means many different things to different people and often poses problems for minorities. Even agreeing upon a system for seeking agreement (making decisions) is problematic. Foucault's formulation of 'the truth of power' as opposed to 'the power of truth' has not been overcome despite the best efforts of Habermas, the dialecticians and educational action researchers.

What of action research without its critical theory grounding? Can lecturers in higher education undertake practical ('technical') action research without regard to ideology critique or changing the world? Of course they can, and indeed it is quite likely that useful 'local' projects of this nature represent the majority of action research undertakings.[7] These projects should not escape critique in terms of the values and ideologies within which they are located, and very often they display the instrumental values of efficiency and effectiveness associated with the 'improvement' and 'rationality' of the Enlightenment. The point is that what constitutes improvement in teaching and learning, and whether or not this leads into a discussion of what should constitute a better community or a better world, is contestable and should be protected from capture and the drive to conformity of a particular world-view.

Contestability and a refusal to curtail criticism should be hallmarks of our staff development endeavours in the face of reassurances that a particular position or approach leads to better education, better staff development, or a better world. The social theory which reached its zenith in Marxism has always attracted a crusading zeal, and the current form of this sees action research as the panacea for academic staff development. In a recent book, Zuber-Skerritt (1992: 122) suggests that:

Through systematic, controlled action research, higher education teachers can become more professional, more interested in pedagogical aspects of higher education, and more motivated to integrate their research and teaching interests in a holistic way. This would in turn lead to greater job satisfaction, better academic programmes, improvement of student learning, and practitioners' insights and contributions to the advancement of knowledge in higher education.

While this might be true for some it needs to be balanced against the legitimate concerns which others might have concerning the ontology, epistemology, methodology and lineage of action research based upon critical theory. It is when the clarion call sounds that our (truly) critical sensibilities should be alerted.

Action research in higher education *must* consist of a *group* process of *rational* reflection generating a critique of the social and educational milieu in which the members operate. For the aim of action research is not only the improvement of learning, teaching and professional development, but also the improvement of the social context in which this personal and professional development takes place.

(Zuber-Skerritt 1992: 122, emphasis added)

Such pronouncements need to be questioned. Why *must* action research consist of a *group* process, and what does *rational* reflection mean? Is there no possibility that we might agree to disagree about local politics, national politics or social policy, and still work together to improve teaching? And even if we do broadly agree on matters of social policy, is it not possible for us to argue legitimately for the emancipatory value of quite different approaches to teaching and learning?

The example provided by Whitehead (1991) may be argued as a challenge to the privileging of group over individual. He has shown how an action research approach may be applied to an individual, in fact, to oneself:

I believe that the incorporation of 'I' as a living contradiction in explanations for the educational development of individuals, has distinguished an original contribution to the action research movement ... I experience problems or concerns when some of my values are denied in my practice; I imagine ways of improving my practice and choose a course of action; I act and gather evidence which will enable me to make a judgement on the effectiveness of my actions; I evaluate the outcomes of my actions; I modify my concerns, ideas and action in the light of my evaluation.

(Whitehead 1991: 94)

The point should also be made that early members of the Frankfurt school were intensely interested in psychoanalytical (intra-individual) analysis. Indeed, the link between this level of analysis and group-based action may be clearly seen:

> critical theory was strongly influenced by psychoanalysis; the analyst assisting in the emancipation of the individual from seemingly un-knowable complexes being mirrored at the social level by the critical theorist facilitating the emancipation of groups from oppressive but unknown or poorly understood ideologies.
>
> (Webb 1991: 40)

It would be perfectly feasible to take action research along a number of paths, including the psychoanalytical or the aesthetic, both of which were of interest to early Frankfurt School writers. The point here is not that this would in some way 'correct' the 'errant' ways of Habermas, Carr and Kemmis, or Zuber-Skerritt, but again, that the issue is contestable. However, some alternative approaches would help to counter a tendency to identify those on the side of the 'good' with those who follow a particular and somewhat narrow interpretation.

There are yet more interpretations. For example, it is possible to 'decon-struct' what is meant by individuals and groups in learning situations as the categories have a habit of escaping the limits which define them (see Webb 1992b). While some may argue that a group is something more than the individuals it includes, each individual is unique, special and can change the nature of the group by his or her participation. It is hard to think 'group' other than abstractly. For example, in thinking of a particular group of students or staff one sees individuals and remembers specific exchanges with oneself and with others. A group is always a group of something (such as students) and it is these 'somethings' which we remember. On the other hand, it is also a mistake to regard the individual as the essential unit – in terms of learning, for example. Students talk about what they are doing (learning) to the person sitting next to them in class, to their flatmates, to their friends, spouses, grown-up sons and daughters, etc. In collaborative projects they share and discuss ideas and talk these over with the teacher. Their identities are formed in the flow of history and society. In what sense is their learning individual?

Apart from the privileging of the group over the individual in action research, the meaning of *rationality* may also be questioned. At one level this repeats the questions already raised concerning whether legitimate differences of opinion on what constitutes progress can be allowed and how one moves forward in the face of disagreement. At another level, however, the concept of rationality itself has been argued as being disempowering and anti-emancipatory.

In what has proved to be an influential paper on 'the repressive myths of critical pedagogy', Ellsworth (1989: 297) suggests that: 'critical pedagogy ... has developed along a highly abstract and utopian line which does not necessarily sustain the daily workings of the education its supporters advocate.' In attempting to teach a course following the tenets of critical pedagogy (including such things as 'classroom analysis and rejection of oppression, injustice, inequality, silencing of marginalized voices, and . . . authoritarian social structures') she took the position of a ' "radical" educator who recognizes and helps students to recognize and name injustice, who empowers students to act against their own and others' oppressions, . . . who criticizes and transforms her or his own understanding in response to the understandings of students' (Ellsworth 1989: 300). This approach to the theory and practice of critical pedagogy comes from leading writers in the field.[8]

But the very admonition that critical pedagogy should encourage rational debate of educational and social issues ignores the fact that the teacher and students enter a course 'with investments of privilege and struggle already made in favor of some ethical and political positions . . . and against other positions' (Ellsworth 1989: 301). The idea that through rational debate the structured differences which inhabit society may be brought to consensus is in line with Habermasian thought but antithetical to what has come to be called 'post-structuralism'. Post-structuralism has now 'amassed overwhelming evidence of the extent to which the myths of the ideal rational person and the "universality" of propositions have been oppressive to those who are not European, White, male, middle class, Christian, able-bodied, thin, and heterosexual' (Ellsworth 1989: 304).

To some extent, the idea of the rational, voluntary individual so despised by critical action researchers has simply been recycled in the idea of the rational, voluntary group. But rational argument serves the interests of those who have the power to form and define rationality, and power imbalances permeate society. For example, the power imbalance between teacher and student (or between staff developer and staff member) has never been satisfactorily addressed:

> theorists of critical pedagogy have failed to launch any meaningful analysis of or program for reformulating the institutionalized power imbalances between themselves and their students, or of the essentially paternalistic project of education itself. In the absence of such an analysis and program, their efforts are limited to trying to transform negative effects of power imbalances within the classroom into positive ones. Strategies such as student empowerment and dialogue give the illusion of equality while in fact leaving the authoritarian nature of the teacher/ student relationship intact.
>
> (Ellsworth 1989: 306)

Ellsworth looks at the notion of 'voice' in allowing students to express their experiences and understandings. Feminism has used this strategy as a means for allowing women to formulate language and concepts in terms of their own understandings or self-definitions and oppositional to the constructions of others. It has been argued, similarly, that teachers may encourage their students to find their authentic voices. But the structural problems remain. How does the well-educated, middle-class, white teacher contribute to the emancipation of her working-class, black, female students?

Attempting to teach according to critical pedagogy (or forming an action research group) assumes that by a rational process of dialogue and sharing of experiences a unity of purpose will be forged and a common understanding of oppression gained. Counter to this, Ellsworth argues that a unified understanding is an undesirable fiction and that each one of us has the ability to be both oppressor and oppressed. She quotes Minh-ha – 'There are no social positions exempt from becoming oppressive to others ... any group – any position – can move into the oppressor role' – and Mary Gentile – 'everyone is someone else's "Other"'' (Ellsworth 1989: 322).

We have thus moved a long way from the Marxist formulation of economically based oppression of the proletariat by the bourgeoisie, from the essentialist feminist position that to be male is to be the oppressor of the female and from similar formulations according to disability, race or sexual orientation. As Chisholm (1990: 253, 255) points out:

> Whilst some of us, as feminists ... can legitimately claim membership of [a] relevant oppressed group, we are, at the same time, class-privileged – and where young people are involved, we have the privilege of adulthood. Therefore, our identities are multiple and contradictory; and we are inevitably bound up in power relationships which we should not be able to afford to deny ... I propose that we begin by not kidding ourselves: about what is achievable in action research; that we know and understand what emancipatory action is; about the elusive character of symmetrical research relations.

Even those representing the standard of privilege (according to Ellsworth the young, white, heterosexual, Christian, able-bodied, thin, middle-class, English-speaking male) may be oppressed by the expectations which their families and society hold of them – they may strive to resist such expectations and attempts to inscribe them with 'essential' characteristics.

There are implications in all of this for staff development informed by critical theory and pursued by action research. If critical theory has failed to take sufficient account of the imbalance which must always persist in educational encounters, then it is unrealistic to base classroom practice on the utopian concept that by equally empowered, rational debate a way will be found through to the empowerment of all. Put simply, there can never be an assurance that the interests of all are in common, or will remain in common. There is thus every chance of 'the interests of all' becoming, in fact, the interests of the most powerful. In an action research setting, the interests of the most powerful may easily be recast as the interests of the best informed ('knowledge is power'), those with a wider and more generalizable knowledge of educational matters or of the action research process itself. This is exactly the position of power which the staff developer can occupy. Chisholm (1990) also predicts that the interests of 'action' and 'research' may work in parallel rather than in collaboration or synthesis. We should not be too surprised, then, if staff developers rather than 'shop-floor' academics are seen as the 'seeders' of action research projects and the main publishers of action research reports.

Conclusion

There is no doubt at all that action research projects can effect good educational developments. Participation in action research groups can also be stimulating for those involved, including developers. However, this chapter has argued that a healthy scepticism and retention of our critical faculty is needed against the ebullient claims and drive to conformity of critical theorists and action researchers. It has also opened the area of multiple claims to understanding which is indicative of postmodernity. In the next chapter this area is examined in a little more detail.

Notes

1. Hegel adopted the word 'dialectic' from Plato's dialogues, which he saw as epitomizing the process of taking what is right from each side of a discussion (thesis, antithesis) in order to form a new position (synthesis) containing the truth of both.
2. The headquarters of the Institute moved to Columbia University in New York in 1934, though some of its original members joined other institutions in the United States.
3. For a compilation of readings by these and other leading first-generation critical theorists, see Bronner and Kellner (1989).
4. An outline of the theory of knowledge in terms of human interests is given in the appendix of Habermas (1971). The theory of communicative action is presented in Habermas (1984; 1987b). Good commentaries on Habermas are McCarthy (1978) and Roderick (1986). A good and accessible introduction to Habermas can be found in Carr and Kemmis (1986).
5. For example 'correspondence theory' suggested a simple, deterministic relationship between education and the needs of corporate capitalism (see Bowles and Gintis 1976; Apple 1979).
6. Accounts of the history of action research are given in Kemmis and McTaggart (1988a) and Zuber-Skerritt (1992). A collection of papers representing this history is to be found in Kemmis and McTaggart (1988b).
7. Weeks and Scott (1992) and Kember and Kelly (1994) give accounts which illustrate many such action research projects in higher education.

8. There is a large literature on the way in which critical theory informs the analysis of educational practices and from which prescriptions for 'critical pedagogy' are said to follow. Paulo Freire, Henry Giroux and Michael Apple are leading names in this area. The writing is directed primarily at school-level education, but much of it may also be used as a critique of higher education. Falmer Press has published a number of books inducting new teachers into the area of critical pedagogy, and some of these may be of some interest to the staff developer. Examples are Popkewitz (1987), Smyth (1987) and the *Wisconsin Series of Teacher Education* including Beyer (1988) and Ginsburg (1988).

5

Postmodernity and Staff Development: Nowhere to Run

The endless cycle of idea and action,
Endless invention, endless experiment,
Brings knowledge of motion, but not of stillness ...
(Eliot 1952: 96, quoted in Yeaman 1994: 70)

Introduction

In thinking about how to open this chapter, an experience I had over 20 years ago in Northern Ireland came to mind. I was walking alone, many miles from a road or settlement, in the highlands of County Antrim. The ground was squelchy, the day was cold and gloomy, and a light, misty rain was falling. Without realizing what had happened I suddenly found myself standing in a peat bog. The mossy vegetation gave little clue of where the land was firm and where it was not. As I stood still, I began to sink. I saw a clump of grass nearby and managed to pull myself out of the hole into which I was disappearing, and gained the new ground. No sooner had I done this, than the new ground began to sink away under my feet. And so it went on. Time and again a new piece of land looked like it would offer safety, stability, a firm foundation. Time and again, once attained, the new ground proved as disappointing as the last. My apprehension increased as I continued to flounder in the bog. I could now see the whole bog moving with each step I took. I was stranded on a raft which moved in waves all around me. I was by this time desperate to find some firm ground where I could feel secure, where I could rest in safety to contemplate the problem.

Eventually, of course, I gained some firm ground and from there was able to find my way out of the bog. The memory of having no firm ground to stand on remains, however, and I find the metaphor appropriate to describe the area we will enter in this chapter – postmodernity. The secure ground, the solid foundations of the past, have been found wanting and have been abandoned. For many, the bedrock of religious belief has shattered; faith in rationality and the ability of science to answer all important questions has been challenged; the possibility of understanding forged in a common humanity has been eroded by inequality and power; and the prospect of social revolution providing for universal social justice has been forsaken. The grand organizing principle is an endangered species. Nowhere, it seems, is there 'firm ground' upon which to stand, and this applies to the theory and practice of staff and educational development, as to everything else. There is no anchoring point, no solid foundation – nowhere to run, nowhere to hide. This is the philosophical landscape of postmodernity, which, according to my scene setting, is perilous and forbidding. On the other hand, the landscape may be seen more positively as offering exciting and liberating prospects for freeing ourselves from the chains of our myopic theories. Postmodernity can liberate us, allow us to shake off our bonds and join with others suffering from different but equally debilitating constraints upon our thoughts and actions. Whether one takes a negative or positive stance towards postmodernity depends, among other things, upon the favour with which one holds modernity. This makes a good starting point.

Modernity and postmodernity

The search for universal truth has a long history, but its latest manifestation is in the period and ideas which are characterized by the term 'modernity'.[1] We have already come across the main elements of modernity in Chapter 2. Modernity may be equated with the most recent stage of the Enlightenment. The essential idea is that individuals can come to know the real world by rational enquiry (for example as science or analytical philosophy). There is constant progress towards the truth about reality as more knowledge is discovered and better explanations are advanced. Scientific explanation is universal because facts are facts and truth is truth, irrespective of who discovers them or in what context. Similarly, ethical, aesthetical, political, legal, social and educational problems can all be addressed by rational enquiry. And the rational enquirer is an autonomous, free-thinking individual.

This is not to say that there is unanimity on the way forward. Positivism, liberalism, Marxism, hermeneutics, humanism, social Darwinism, Freudianism, essentialist feminism and others claim a fundamental insight concerning the way towards individual or social progress. Each offers a 'meta-narrative', a 'grand narrative', a 'foundational discourse': a major organizing principle of explanation. Postmodernity[2] finds it impossible to accept total theories such as these.

Lyotard (1984) describes postmodernism as the rejection of 'grand narratives' or any form of totalizing thought. Lyotard sees the spread of computers and information technology generally as being integrally linked with the diffusion of knowledge to local levels. Knowledge will become more localized, specific, diverse and contingent. 'Grand narratives' become obsolete, and in their place, as Giroux (1989: 10) puts it, 'postmodernism appears as an ideological and political marker for referencing a world without stability, a world where knowledge is constantly changing and where meaning can no longer be anchored in a teleological view of history'. Giroux (1989: 18) quotes from Stanley Aronowitz a passage which sums up much postmodern thought:

> Postmodern thought . . . is bound to discourse, literally narratives about the world that are admittedly partial. Indeed, one of the crucial features of discourse is the intimate tie between knowledge and interest, the latter being understood as a 'standpoint' from which to grasp 'reality.' Putting these terms in inverted commas signifies that will to abandon scientificity, science as a set of propositions claiming validity by any given competent investigatory. What postmodernists deny is precisely this category of impartial competence. For competence is constituted as a series of exclusions – of women, of people, of colour, of nature as a historical agent, of the truth value of art.

In the postmodern condition we, as educators and staff developers, would acknowledge each of the preceding chapters with its interpretation of what educational and staff development looks like from the standpoints of positivism, hermeneutics and critical theory, we would accept each as a 'grand' or 'meta' narrative, and dismiss the totalizing effect that the acceptance of any one would imply. Conceiving of phenomenography, reflective practice or action research as supplying the theoretical blueprint for practice would be seen as delusory. The staff developer in a postmodern world would retain the flexibility to step from one to the other. The view or theory adopted by the developer would depend upon the interests of the developer and the demands of the local context. Since there is no grand, unifying theory, the postmodern staff developer would also be very interested in the position of those claiming to articulate such theory. For example, how does one become a 'competent' and 'qualified' phenomenographer, reflective practitioner or action researcher, and how is power used to exclude other interests and voices? As no grand narrative can represent the 'truth' about educational and staff development, a pragmatic approach is indicated. The flexibility which this affords might well be regarded as of distinct advantage. However, flexibility also comes at a price.

Structuralism

As a way of introducing post-structuralism, it might also be appropriate to say something about structuralism. The foundation of structuralism lies in Ferdinand de Saussure's structural linguistics. Lecturing in Geneva shortly after the turn of the century, Saussure attempted to show how 'the world' becomes present to us. In order to do this he suggested that we know 'the world' through language and language works through words (the signifiers) referring to concepts (the signified). For example, the words 'staff development' are signifiers of something. Other words could originally have been chosen instead of 'staff development', and in different languages different words *are* used. No particular formation of words is 'right' or 'correct', the important thing is the understanding of the relationship between the signifiers (the words 'staff development') and the signified (the concept or idea of staff development). Saussure referred to this relationship as the 'sign'.

He did not go one step further and suggest that the sign corresponded to an object of reality; the concept 'staff development' does not correspond to a real object and nor do the signifiers 'table', 'woman', 'molecule', 'day', 'teacher'. None of these has an existence outside of a sign system, and it is the system which gives each its meaning. Deriving the value and meaning of a particular element from its place within a system is a central tenet of all structuralist thought. Each element is defined and understood not of itself, but by its relationship with the other elements.

In language, for example, the meaning of a particular word is not apparent from the word itself, but from its position in a sentence. Change this position or modify the surrounding words, and without in anyway altering the original word, its value is modified. And if language can only be understood by understanding the relationships among words, the fundamental distinction is between 'being something' or 'not being something'. Seung (1982), quoted in Cherryholmes (1988: 10), puts it thus:

> Binary distinction is the simplest logical device for discrimination, namely between having a quality or attribute and not having it, or between belonging to a class and not belonging to it. It underlies every assertion or denial. There can be no more pervasive logical principle than this one.

Some words are thought of as opposites (day/night; woman/man) but most are binary distinctions (woman/girl; teacher/student). In structural analysis the side of the binary distinction which is more valued in the structural system usually appears first (man/woman; teaching/learning; teacher/student). It was in the mounting of a critique of this structural analysis of language that post-structuralism developed.

Post-structuralism, Derrida and deconstruction

Lying within the general domain of postmodernity, post-structuralism[3] refers specifically to the critique of structural arguments originating in linguistics but now apparent in many academic disciplines. Jacques Derrida,[4] in particular, has mounted a critique of structural thought that has reverberated throughout the halls of the academy. He is concerned principally with written texts, but his argument applies to texts of all kinds. He claims that the meaning in (or of) a text is not given in the binary oppositions, distinctions or categorizations in the text. A text may be read in many different ways and different meanings may be ascribed to it. The *reader* thus becomes crucial in deciding the meaning of the text, and multiple readings are possible.

This is so because the words of the text (the signifiers) and the concepts, ideas and definitions to which they refer are not bonded together; their relationship is infinitely expandable. If we want to understand the word 'teach', for example, the *Oxford English Dictionary* suggests a range of definitions including:

> To show ... to point in a particular direction ... to show by way of information or instruction ... to impart or convey the knowledge of ... to give instructions or lessons in ... to make known ... to communicate ... to inform ... to educate ... to train ... to school ... to let a person know the cost or penalty of something ...

Now suppose we take some of these words and look them up. Do 'information' and 'instruction' have the same meaning? And what about 'impart' and 'convey'; 'instructions' and 'lessons'; 'make known', 'communicate', 'inform', 'educate,' 'train' and 'school'? To obtain a definition of any one of these terms we will have to look it up and for each one we will find an equally long list of definitional words. And so it continues, on and on. Derrida claims that we can never determine meaning by definition, as this is a fundamentally open process. The signifiers become the signified which in turn become the signifiers once more. As Sarup (1989: 35) puts it, 'signifiers and signified are continually breaking apart and reattaching in new combinations, thus revealing the inadequacy of Saussure's model of the sign'. In making sense or taking meaning from a text, the reader is constantly looking for *difference* in establishing a word as different from others, and in doing this the reader constantly postpones or *defers* ascribing meaning as the play of signification does not allow a final convergence or closure. Derrida brings these two strategies together in the formulation he calls *différance* (the endless 'differing' and 'deferring' ingrained in any attempt to find meaning). This formulation also encapsulates the way that meaning is produced in space (differ) and time (defer).

Through the 'deconstruction' of a text, Derrida has provided a way of undermining the 'apparent' or 'common-sense' meaning which may be ascribed to the text, and of uncovering hidden meaning. By this method he demonstrates the essential openness of texts and the possibility of multiple readings. In a close reading of a text he examines 'the imperceptible displacements, that might otherwise escape the reader's eye' (Sarup 1989: 56). In order to do this he recasts binary oppositions so that the subordinate term becomes the dominant one. It then becomes apparent that the dominant term owes its place not to logic but to the force of a dominant metaphor which works to exclude or suppress the subordinate term. This method also allows Derrida to challenge the myth of origination in the text by always being able to trace further back (or further forward) than the story in the text allows.

His attack goes to the very basis of philosophy and understanding. The direction of understanding in Western philosophy (from Plato via Descartes to Husserl) has been based on a metaphysic concerned with establishing identity. A thing is what it is. Its identity comes from being what it is and our understanding of it comes from grasping this identity, this essence. The opposite of a thing is inessential, a contamination or abomination. By inverting this metaphysic, Derrida claims that only *différance* produces identity; things of themselves have no identity of their own. Derrida's critique claims that everything can also be 'otherwise' and in fact only has its own identity because of 'the other'. This applies in contexts from the deep cultural binary distinction of man/woman to the most abstract set of mathematical axioms. There are always boundary problems. In terms of gender formation, for example, Epstein and Straub (1992) recognize that rigid binary divisions between masculine and feminine are no more than attempts to control and regulate the 'uncontrollable elasticity and terrifying lack of boundaries within or between human bodies'. Gender ambiguity, transvestism and difference of all kinds are as permanent a feature as the masculine/feminine binary distinction itself. Even a set of mathematical axioms can never make a complete and meaningful system of explanation as there must be a way of dealing with undecided or incomplete elements, and this will require addition to the axioms. This fits well with Gödel's meta-mathematical theorems which suggest that any formal system is 'undecidable' because it generates elements that can be proved to belong to the system and not to belong to the system at the same time.

Similarly, the problems of 'reality' and the language which is used to represent it are equally undecidable:

Descriptive language, no matter how precise and exhaustive, can never succeed in anchoring itself to a reality; it can only move 'sideways' through the realm of words in attempting to do so. . . . The idea(l) that shared language (e.g. definition) reflects a shared reality is an article of faith which unfortunately can only be 'substantiated' in more language and thus not really substantiated at all. The truth of any statement, scientific or otherwise, which ultimately must rely on some anchoring in order to avoid being completely arbitrary, is *undecidable*. *This in turn does not imply that there is no truth, but rather that if there is, we are incapable of pinning it down.*

(Strohmayer and Hannah 1992: 36; emphasis in original)

Derrida's argument thus goes to the heart of the Western tradition of identity. According to Derrida, identity is ultimately undecidable in the movement of language through *différance*. If postmodernism stands for the abandonment of foundational discourses, in his destabilization of the Western metaphysic, Derrida has produced the postmodern abandonment *par excellence*.

What application does this have for educational and staff development? Cherryholmes (1988) offers examples of deconstructing educational icons such as Tyler's rationale, Schwab's 'practical four' and Bloom's taxonomy. Because it has been (and still is) influential in higher education, it may be worthwhile to sketch an outline of the latter. Cherryholmes (1988: 43) points out the necessary conditions for a taxonomy as follows:

> Constructing a taxonomy presumes an underlying structure that can be ordered into a hierarchy of classes and categories. The meaning of each level is determined by differences from and relationships to other levels . . . the categories must be exhaustive (there must be a category for every learning objective) and mutually exclusive (a learning objective can be put in one and only one category).

The categories which Bloom *et al.* (1956) annunciate in the cognitive domain have become well known and well used in educational development. They are knowledge, comprehension, application, analysis, synthesis, and evaluation. Each higher term subsumes the necessary but lower levels. This raises many problems, however, in that evaluation, for example, may be the first step in deciding upon a knowledge objective, and similarly:

> [c]omprehension can also precede knowledge, because if one cannot comprehend, translate, and interpret certain messages, some kinds of knowledge cannot be learned. Likewise, application sometimes precedes comprehension, because only after successful application is comprehension demonstrated.
>
> (Cherryholmes 1988: 45)

The same kind of point can be made with regard to application, analysis and synthesis, so that 'there is no transcendent reason or justification for always putting analysis before synthesis, application before analysis, comprehension before application, or knowledge before comprehension' (Cherryholmes 1988: 46). (It may be noted in passing that a conception of learning in terms more synonymous with hermeneutical circles would avoid these problems.)

A critique of phenomenography

The notions of 'deep' and 'surface' approaches .o learning are another part of the modern educational development can on. The theory of knowledge and methodology which produced them is called phenomenography. The aim of phenomenography is 'to find and systematize forms of thought in terms of which people interpret aspects of reality' (Marton 1981: 180). It is 'a research method for mapping the qualitatively different ways in which people experience, conceptualize, perceive, and understand various aspects of, and phenomena in, the world around them' (Marton 1986: 31).

Having its greatest impact in Sweden, the United Kingdom and Australia, phenomenography has played an important role in suggesting to educational developers an agenda for researching and viewing educational practice. Reference to 'deep' and 'surface' approaches to learning (Marton and Säljö 1976; Marton *et al.* 1984) has become commonplace and nowadays forms the basis for institutional policy concerning goals for teaching and learning. A 'deep' approach to learning is one in which a person tries to understand and construct meaning from a learning event – such as reading a passage from a book. A person using a 'surface' process does not see past the text to the sense and meaning of the passage – that person simply tries to remember the text. It has been in the attempt to move students from surface to deep approaches, mainly by having them more actively involved in learning, that popular series of teaching tips (such as Gibbs *et al.* 1987) are based.

While seeing some utility in the general direction of this thinking, and while accepting as beneficial some of the prescriptions suggested, I believe that there are some difficulties with both phenomenography and the directions for teaching which follow from phenomenographic studies. I also find the lack of contest and criticism in this area over such a long period quite puzzling. It is as though we have found a theory to support our deepest prejudices and common-sense opinions, and thus seek to cherish and protect it.

It is hardly surprising that Husserl's name crops up from time to time in the phenomenographic literature as Husserl was the founder of modern phenomenology. His object was to show how 'the mind took possession of experience, relating thought to the object-of-thought through an act of structured perception' (Norris 1982: 44). Again, Husserl's phenomenology attempts to draw the distinction between the 'basic, constitutive structures of perception from the mass of indeterminate or "merely" subjective experience' (Norris 1982: 43). Husserl believed perception of phenomena to be possible without the contaminating effects of history and intellectual experience. The apprehension of phenomena at the purest level is a direct experiential and perceptual encounter in contrast to normal thought structures (including logic) which belong to the expressive or representational realm. Derrida's critique of Husserl shows how perception is always already representation and that it is impossible to have 'a primordial intuition' separate from language or other cultural systems.

Phenomenography differs from phenomenology in that it considers only the 'second-order' or conceptual thoughts of people. Phenomenography attempts to aggregate 'modes of experience . . . forms of thought' (Marton 1981: 181) into a limited number of categories. Phenomenographers do not claim to study 'what is there' in the world (reality) but they do claim to study 'what is there' in people's conceptions of the world. In so doing, they are not perhaps so far removed from the Husserlian idea of pristine perception and of the ability to 'bracket' one's own socially and historically 'contaminated' conceptual apparatus, as they might think. In other words, how does phenomenography take into account the historical and social construction of thought? Are phenomenographers simply reporting the history of a particular discipline as they find it in the people they interview? What categories do they build to house people's conceptions other than the categories of their own historically and socially informed understanding? Derrida would, of course, point to the act of interpretation (the categories and commentaries of the researchers) as the telling part of the story. The idea that these are 'simply' reported or 'simply there' in some way outside the historical and social experience of the reporters, would not be taken seriously. Deconstruction would also point to the different interpretative readings which could be made from the basic data and to the subtexts which a reading of phenomenographic commentaries might reveal.

In practice, phenomenographic studies often see students being asked to describe their understanding of a concept, a text or a situation, with the researcher then sorting the descriptions into a 'handful' (in fact surprisingly often five) categories based upon 'the most distinctive characteristics . . . structurally significant differences' (Marton 1986: 34). Invariably one of the categories displays 'correct meaning, correct knowledge or correct understanding', while the others are recapitulations of earlier, now supposedly discredited accounts. The 'authorized' conception is the one which is in accordance with 'the standpoint of modern science' and those who have been identified as having aberrant forms of understanding may then be helped to the correct view: 'A careful account of the different ways people think about phenomena may help uncover conditions that facilitate the transition from one way of thinking to a qualitatively "better" perception of reality' (Marton 1986: 36).

We have already seen in Chapter 2 that there is no possibility of observation outside theory or predetermined understanding. In Chapter 3 we saw the historicity of understanding and the importance of 'prejudice': 'We are always understanding and interpreting in light of our anticipatory prejudgments and prejudices, which are themselves changing in the course of history' (Bernstein 1983: 139). This leaves phenomenographic explanation with a problem: that of simply *reproducing the discourse* of which it is a part. If the researcher is always already embedded in a tradition of understanding, and if it is not possible simply to interpret and categorize without recourse to prior understanding, then it seems likely that phenomenographic research will come up with findings which could have been predicted at the outset. And this is what happens. Taylor (1993) comments upon it in his important paper on the implications of hermeneutics for higher education practice. He notes how a phenomenographic analysis of foreign language learning came up with the two conceptions – structural and communicative – which have been in dispute since the days of the Greeks, and comments that 'it is curious that phenomenographic analyses of differing conceptions tend to tell us much the same as we can discover by studying the history of attitudes toward the subject in question' (Taylor 1993: 63).

As to the 'correctness' of a particular conception, this is not always as clear as a phenomenographic researcher might suggest. Taylor uses an example from a phenomenographic approach to the concept of price in economics (Dahlgren and Marton 1978; Dahlgren 1984). The 'correct' conception of price is as a function of supply and demand, whereas an aberrant conception is that price is a function of the cost of production. But this latter conception is actually very close to the labour theory of value developed by Marx and used in Marxist economics as an important bridge between social and political philosophy and economic policy. It was also commonplace in early classical economic theory. Whether the conception is 'correct' or not does not therefore lie in the conception itself, but in the interpretation of the researcher.

In a similar example, Säljö (1988) observes two conceptions of evolution: that the environment affects evolutionary adaptation, and that adaptation is random. He observes that 'it is worth remarking, in passing, that in this particular context the two conceptions of evolution have a close similarity with the historically well known difference between a Lamarckian explanation of evolution and a (neo-) Darwinian' (Säljö 1988: 41). We are told that the Lamarckian version is no longer accepted. Despite this it keeps reappearing because, as with many aberrant conceptions, it is easier to understand, more 'natural', more commonsensical. It is a thorn in the side of the instructor as it is 'resistant to change', and 'even after exposure to explicit instruction, many students keep to the Lamarckian version' (Säljö 1988: 41). In fact the position is not quite so clear. There is still considerable debate concerning what constitutes Darwinian, neo-Darwinian, Lamarckian and neo-Lamarckian positions, at what levels, in what contexts, and with what interpretative possibilities (see, for example, Morss 1990).

I believe that education should be about the contest of ideas and the means by which judgements are challenged. Alternative views are its lifeblood, and the ability to marshal arguments for and against propositions and positions, its stock in trade. The power of truth should continually be forged in every classroom. It should not be so easily confined to 'what is accepted'. What is accepted, in all branches of knowledge, may owe more to the truth of power: the weight of institutionalized and embedded interests in perpetuating a particular research programme or paradigm. For example, it is not so long ago that the results of qualitative research in education were dismissed as inconsequential. More recently still, the idea that a researcher can legitimately follow a political agenda would have been questioned, and the knowledge claims made from this perspective queried. The discipline changes by critique and contest, and we should wish to see a sense of scepticism and challenge in our students. This is somewhat different from an attitude which says 'trust me, I already know the right answers'.

Phenomenography occupies a curious position in terms of epistemology. It rejects Husserlian phenomenology but, in its failure to 'screen out' the historical experience of the researcher, simply repeats the same mistake at the next level. It claims an orientation towards human subjectivity and qualitative (rather than quantitative) methods, yet is method-driven in an attempt to make the kind of generalization associated with positive science. There is little of the hermeneutical spirit of openness to the other, mutual respect and the expectation of change in *both* conversationalists. The conversation is uneven as one of the parties thinks that they already know the right answer. This not a very satisfactory model from which to construe either educational or staff development relationships. One is left with the feeling that phenomenographic research will continue to find confirmation of its suspicions as it continues to reproduce the discourses in which it is embedded. We should not be surprised that, in Taylor's (1993: 64) phrase, 'ontography recapitulates historiography'.

The 'deep' and 'surface' literature also exhibits many of the features which attracted Derrida's attention in other areas. The privileged term comes first and describes all that is 'good' and 'worthy' in learning. The surface approach to learning is generally despised: it is the realm of those unfortunates caught in time warps such as Aristotelian rather than Newtonian physics; neo-Lamarckian rather than neo-Darwinian evolution; Marxist, Christian or early capitalist economics rather than neo-classical economics. It is the domain of the unfortunates who learn by rote, who repeat things over and over, who memorize acronyms and use all kinds of devices in order that they (we?) can remember. They have mistaken learning the signifier (the words, symbols, representations) for learning the signified (the concept, the idea). Derrida would of course have none of this, and would claim signifier and signified to be in the constant and indeterminate play of *différance*.

That, at least is the normal case. However, in Marton *et al.* (1993) we find one of the few phenomenographic studies which begins to question basic concepts, rather than simply reproducing in differing settings the standard notions of 'deep' and 'surface' approaches to learning. It is an interesting paper in a number of ways, one being the attempt to step outside of the Western tradition which has been the usual (and espoused) area of interest for phenomenography.

'Truth' in phenomenography has been conceived in a scientific consensus way: it is what most scientists think it is at the moment. 'Truth' and the 'right answer' to the problems which they ask students to tackle are usually synonymous; the right and proper way to get to the truth is through a 'deep' approach to learning. (Examples of 'deep' approaches to learning leading to 'untruthful' propositions and wrong answers are in short supply.) The meta-narrative is that the understanding of the Western tradition (the Enlightenment) has produced truthful propositions; that the 'deep' approach epitomizes this tradition and that it is our job as teachers to foster these sound habits of mind in our students and thus perpetuate the tradition. The alignment is essentially conservative and reinforcing of 'consensus' or status quo positions and understanding. This all stands more chance of acceptance when concepts or problems, like a number of those chosen by phenomenographers, come from (Newtonian) physics and are set in Western society.

But what if we do not accept this version of the Western tradition and valorize instead the rhetorical nature of truth; what if a non-Western tradition valorizes a 'surface' approach to learning? Is all 'surface' learning bad? What of the many thousands of years humankind has spent learning by ritual chanting (prayer; times-tables), what of the oral histories, genealogies and mantras learned and passed on by repetition? Can we have no respect for such learning, and are we obliged to lead all those who engage in it from the error of their ways? And what if surface learning approaches actually produce high academic achievement? Then, surely, phenomenography has a problem.

It is exactly this problem which is examined by Marton *et al.* (1993) in the 'paradox of the Chinese learner'. The solution turns out to be that the binary notion of 'deep' and 'surface' is too crude because Chinese learners use 'surface' (rote, memorizing) strategies, but for 'deep' (understanding) purposes. The following appears at the end of the paper under the subtitle 'Solving the paradox of the Chinese learner'.

> In Western countries memorization and rote learning are generally equated and it is commonly believed that they do not lead to understanding. A new way of seeing the relationship between memorization and understanding as being intertwined was identified in this study. In addition, a distinction was found *within* memorization, rather than *between* memorization and understanding. These results enable us to see that the traditional Asian practice of repetition or memorization can have different purposes. On the one hand, repetition can be associated with mechanical rote learning. On the other hand, memorization through repetition can be used to deepen and develop understanding. If memorization is understood in this latter way, the paradox of the Chinese learner is solved.
>
> (Marton *et al.* 1993: 15–16)

While Marton *et al.* highlight (in italics) the assertion that the distinction between memorization and understanding should remain, it seems clear that a surface approach to learning can at the same time be a deep one.

Here we are back once more in the territory of Derrida. The valorized term (deep approach) is usually seen as the entity, the identity, whereas the secondary term (surface approach) is the abomination. Derrida shows that identity is constructed through *différance*, and the seeds of the secondary term pervade the primary. In the binary opposition of 'deep' and 'surface' itself lies the occasion for the deconstructive reading. The following reference to phenomenology stands true for phenomenography:

> the intelligible meaning, which (according to phenomenology) tran-
> scends, precedes, and determines a text and stands outside the play of
> sensible linguistic representation, is itself possible only on the occasion
> of the text and is itself caught up in a web of references that constitutes
> another text. The intelligible, which phenomenology would want to
> privilege as a realm apart, is itself inscribed in the sensible and in the
> indefinite texture of reference.
>
> (Ryan 1982: 22)

It is also interesting to note that paradox, a device used for illuminating and extending the possibilities of binary (linear, rational) thought, is also much used in postmodernity. In the postmodern condition, there is a realization that the 'solution' of a paradox will depend on the assertion of power by a predominant discourse. In short, paradoxes are posed for illumination, they are not posed to be 'solved'.

This also raises the question of the nature of truth and logic in Derrida, who, it should be readily admitted, constructs logical analyses and arguments in making claims to truth. It is a similar point to the larger assertion that postmodernity, in claiming the end of foundational discourses, meta- or grand narratives, is no more than a foundational discourse itself. Derrida's response is that he is constantly concerned with the problem of using the devices and materials of the work which he seeks to question. This is plain to see in his use of *sous rature*, which may be taken to mean 'under erasure'. Martin Heidegger used the device in his attempts to grapple with 'Being'. For Heidegger, Being could not be contained by the word. He would therefore write 'Being', put a cross through it, and leave the crossed-out word in the text. By so doing he intended to draw attention to his argument that Being comes before and goes beyond representation or signification: Being is the 'transcendental signified' which is impossible of representation. Derrida uses the device similarly, to show that by writing a word and leaving it visible, the word is necessary, but the cross placed through the word subverts, displaces and points to its weakness. This illustrates Derrida's greater aim of pointing to the insufficiency of representation, logic and a particular perspective on truth, while using these very devices to make the point.

   Much of the coinage of educational and staff development could benefit from *sous rature*. Consider some of the words we routinely use: teaching, learning, teacher, student, lecturer, lecture, tutorial, laboratory, university, knowledge, understanding, memory, information. Any one of these could provoke a book entitled 'The idea of (the). . . .'. Indeed, it is my belief as an educational and staff developer that the linguistic/language area of research in our discourse will experience some growth over the next few years. For too long have we assumed that language is neutral and that our understandings of the discourse are in common. As the area develops and insights of postmodernism come into their own, the importance of the 'linguistic turn' and the work of Derrida will become more apparent. It may also be that we turn to the consideration and interpretation of our own history.

Foucault and History

   We are members of a higher education development community which defines what is appropriate, current and valid in the field, and from which we absorb guidelines as to the nature, scope and purpose of our own endeavours. In Foucauldian terms, we are part of an anonymous discourse which pre-dates our own arrival on the scene, and which moulds and constrains our agency as individuals.

                                                              (Webb 1992a: 351)

Normal histories trace development from a point in the past through to the present. They tend to suggest the inevitability of what has happened and discard as 'detail' elements which do not confirm the central story. Michel Foucault[5] wrote rather different histories, if histories they were at all.[6] Before his death in 1984, Foucault wrote a series of books concerning the development of discourses which made specific social practices possible. A discourse is a 'network of practices which systematically form the objects of which they speak' (Foucault 1972: 49). For example, educational and staff developers use words in their writings, conferences, workshops, etc., which form the discourse of educational and staff development. However, this is only part of the story because the discourse then forms the educational and staff developers. A discourse is far from being merely words which name objects, thoughts or actions; a discourse has the power to create objects, structure our thoughts and make us what we are.
   Foucault wrote on the development of madness and mental institutions (1965), prisons (1979), hospitals (1973), sexuality (1978), language (1972), knowledge and the human sciences (1970). In each case he attempted to show the reciprocal relationship between discourses and practices. He investigates how discourses come to be, how they motivate action and

produce institutions, and how actions and institutions in turn form, regulate and control discourses. The link between discourse and practice is pervasive. Cherryholmes (1988), for example, usually refers to 'discourse-practice' in order to 'emphasise similarities, reinforcement, interpenetration between the two' (Cherryholmes 1988: 9).

It is perhaps worth noting at this point Foucault's position in terms of the 'structure/agency' issue. Obviously individuals are constrained by the social, political and economic structures of the society into which they are born. They learn to become what the structures they experience (class, gender, religious, educational, marriage, childrearing, etc.) signal to be appropriate. Structures make people. Equally obviously, structures are created by people, they are resisted and changed by people's actions. People make structures. The insight of the hermeneutical circle can again inform this paradox. A close parallel to this is found in Anthony Giddens's (1979) concept of 'structuration'. Instead of the 'either/or' of 'structure/agency', 'structuration' describes the relationship as 'both/and'. Structures both control and provide opportunities for agency, which in turn produces, challenges and changes social structures.

While acknowledging the nature of discourse production and development, Foucault's emphasis is quite clearly on the power of discourses in constraining and regulating human thinking and action. Again, as indicated in the quotation at the beginning of this section, discourses pre-date our arrival as individuals ready to participate in the discourse and they lay the ground rules for what is appropriate, current, acceptable and valid. The origin of these practices and accepted ways of thinking is obscure and anonymous. They do not tend to have a single author or point of origination.

A discourse, such as the higher education development discourse,[7] has a structure defined by power relations. An outline of questions to probe the power relations of a discourse is suggested by Cherryholmes (1988: 107) as follows:

1. Who is authorized to speak?
2. Who listens?
3. What can be said?
4. What remains unspoken?
5. How does one become authorized to speak?
6. What utterances are rewarded?
7. What utterances are punished?
8. Which categories, metaphors, modes of description, explanation, and argument are valued and praised; which are excluded and silenced?
9. What social and political arrangements reward and deprive statements?

So what is the nature of the higher education development discourse? In suggesting responses to these questions I will be deliberately provocative. The higher education development discourse authorizes to speak mainly middle-aged, white, male, heterosexual, senior academic, research-orientated, full-time developers in universities. It authorizes to listen all those developers who do not speak, and those who teach. It allows to be said that which confirms a very small number of development stories (meta-narratives or foundational discourses). What remain unspoken are the development stories of others. The discourse especially values generalizable theory rather than context-specific (subject-orientated) theory. General theory empowers and better serves the interests of staff developers, whereas context-specific theory empowers and serves the interests of subject specialists.

One becomes authorized to speak by gaining entrance to the media of speech, such as academic journals and conferences. The higher the level of access to such media, the greater the necessity to speak a dominant development story. Utterances which are rewarded are those in high academic media which confirm and develop a foundational discourse and bring into direct correspondence the idea of higher education development with a predominant foundational discourse. Utterances which show practical application of a foundational discourse to general educational settings are also rewarded, to a lesser degree. Utterances which are penalized are those which deny the possibility of a general development story (often uttered by teachers) or which are outside predominant foundational discourses. The major categories and metaphors which are valued and praised at present are those of 'reflective practice', the 'deep' and 'surface' metaphor and the idea of emancipation through collaborative action research. Those excluded comprise much of hermeneutics, humanism, post-structuralism including post-structural feminism, ethnically informed, localized and historicized research. The social and political arrangements which reward statements comprise the entire apparatus of power and status associated with appointment to senior university positions.

The point is that in seeking an explanation for the prescriptions of educational and staff development, we can never avoid the nature of their discourse/practice production. For example, the truth concerning what comprises 'good teaching' can never be asserted separately from a discourse/practice. Knowledge is not disinterested, and so when we listen to the theory and practice espoused by staff developers, we might reflect on the question: 'you say this serves my interests, but does it not, more so serve your own?'

Perhaps the main discursive change which developers are presently hoping to achieve is from 'broadcasting' or 'filling empty vessels' metaphors concerned with content, to 'reflective', 'deep' or 'emancipatory' approaches to learning. But if we follow Foucault, the truth we receive about teaching or learning is the product of a spatially and historically situated discourse.

The truth of the discourse is the truth of the power relationships of the discourse. We cannot escape this. We cannot, for example, 'reflect' on our teaching to produce some 'essential' truth about teaching, or an 'authentic' reflective practice. The very words themselves come from the discourse and what they come to mean in action is part of the discourse/practice. Power even moulds what we want to be: power shapes desire. Power, as it is manifest in a discourse, makes the people of the discourse. The only way forward is thus for people to be aware of the power relations of the discourse and to attempt to gain some control of the discourse/practice, rather than accepting and following the views of those most rewarded by the particular power relationships of the discourse. In this regard, the commercialization of the discourse is interesting, too. In short, 'those who sell, win'. The marketing of educational and staff development materials (particularly derivatives from the 'deep' and 'surface' literature) is an area worthy of research, sharing commonality with the work of Apple (1986) in the area of school textbooks.

But the power of control does not end with the powerful of the discourse. Foucault's thesis is that with the end of monarchical power and overt discipline there has been a shift to self-regulation and self-discipline. He illustrates this by referring to the panopticon, which was Jeremy Bentham's idea of a circular prison in which each cell could be observed from the central tower. Prisoners come to police themselves under this system of surveillance. So it is in the modern world, according to Foucault, that control and regulation have passed to individuals and are enforced through surveillance. An interesting question is how far self-regulation by teachers (or departments, or universities), which is argued as being necessary for the accountability of professional practice, in fact acts as a regulatory device against professional interests. There can be no definitive answer to this, the answer being played out in the various local sites of contest. But Foucault's point is that we can never simply base our position on an assertion of what everyone should recognize as 'good', 'truthful', 'professional' or 'accountable'. We cannot say that a good teacher is thus, professional practice is thus, the epitome of the university is thus, a just society is thus. The idea of each of these will be put forward (or resisted) in different societies at different periods by different power interests or relations. Before joining a particular club, we would do well to examine the membership, or more particularly, the non-membership.

Conclusion

What of the criticisms of postmodernism?[8] At a superficial level it has been dismissed as a fad. Of those who have engaged with it seriously, the major criticism has come from social theorists and philosophers of the left. If 'anything goes', if there are no solid foundations upon which to stand, how can social improvement and social justice be affirmed? Postmodernism has thus been argued as an aberration of late capitalism or as a conservative reaction to progressive politics. (Much has also been made of links between some deconstructive writers and fascism.) Put simply, the argument is that there is truth, and it is the truth of exploitation and suffering: the truth of the historical struggle for emancipation. This represents a return to words as objective signifiers of reality, and Strohmayer and Hannah (1992: 41) comment on this as follows:

> Contrary to popular belief, paying heed to the problem of representation does not require one to deny non-textual determination, just to treat with extreme scepticism any claim to have established an 'objective' understanding of 'how it works.'

In other words, we should not let ourselves be duped into accepting an 'objective' account of oppression, exploitation or emancipation. And because we do not accept someone's 'objective' account of the 'reality' of oppression, exploitation or emancipation, this does not mean that we are powerless to act:

> we still would much prefer to have founding principles present themselves to us. We chafe at having to make difficult (because at some level arbitrary) choices on our own. *But, this lack of external guidance does not suddenly transform concern into indifference.* If anything, it makes the unavoidable choices more painful.
>   (Strohmayer and Hannah 1992: 49; emphasis in original)

This is the message of postmodernism generally. It challenges us to move out of our particular comfort zones (reflective practice, action research, phenomenography, etc.). As we articulate our version of what is 'good' as an educational practice, as we espouse our values for education and for staff development, we do so in the knowledge that we are party to the *construction* of difference, the Other, the alternative case. Our horizons and our knowledge are tied to our interests. We are perhaps more wary and critical of the educational and staff development discourse into which we have been inducted. We are interested in the use of language within the discourse and the way that discourse and practice inform each other. We do not lose values or abrogate responsibility, but they become less anchored, more contingent. This does not excuse us from action: postmodernism will not imprison us and prevent us from acting. Indeed, it could help us to see for the first time the imprisoning characteristics of our most cherished standpoints.

Notes

1. 'Modernism' is used to denote a movement in the arts (architecture, visual arts, literature, drama, film) which arose during the present century in opposition to classicism. Classicism expressed unity and continuity, it mirrored reality, it clearly identified people in society and history. Modernism offered a new unity assembled from multiple perspectives, materials and individual style. 'Modernity' includes modernism in the arts but also the ideas of progress towards truth and freedom by rational enquiry and technical problem-solving in science, politics, ethics, sociology, etc. However, modernism has come to be used interchangeably with modernity.
2. Following on from note 1, 'postmodernity' and 'postmodern' are used interchangeably to mean the wide critique of modernity associated with the rejection of 'grand narratives' in science, politics, ethics, sociology, etc. It may also be noted that the term 'postmodern' (along with terms such as 'media society', 'information society', 'consumer society' and 'postindustrial society') has been used as a description of contemporary Western society. For a valiant attempt to bring together many aspects of 'the postmodern condition' (and to ground postmodernity within the contemporary transformation of capitalism), see Harvey (1990).
3. 'Post-structuralism' is used by many writers synonymously with 'postmodernity'. Here it will be used with a narrower meaning to indicate the move away from structuralist thought. This is in line with usages within the broad area of postmodernity which refer to particular critiques such as the post-positivist, post-Marxist, post-feminist.
4. Important original works by Jaques Derrida include Derrida (1973; 1976; 1978). The secondary literature provides an easier introduction: see, for example, Norris (1982) Dews (1987), Cherryholmes (1988) and Sarup (1989).
5. Commentaries on Foucault include those by Dreyfus and Rabinow (1982) and Cousins and Hussain (1984); selected readings include (Foucault 1977; 1980) and Rabinow (1984).
6. Foucault referred to himself as an historian of ideas but called his investigations 'archaeology' or 'genealogy'. Dreyfus and Rabinow (1982) suggest 'interpretive analytics' as a more appropriate term implying the interpretive sense of empathy (understanding, *Verstehen*) together with the interpretive sense of standing apart (distancing) for the purpose of analysis. Whatever the terms used, the important thing is the 'focus on the local, discontinuous, disqualified, illegitimate knowledges . . . there are no constants, no essences, no immobile forms of uninterrupted continuities structuring the past' (Sarup 1989: 64).
7. I am assuming that 'higher education development discourse' or 'educational and staff development discourse' has some meaning. There are obviously 'subdiscourses' to which participants may belong (phenomenography, action research, medical education, student support, etc.) and cleavages according to geographical location.
8. For a further critique of postmodernism in education, see Beyer and Liston (1992).

6

By Diverse Paths:
Developing Staff Developers

I came to my truth by diverse paths and in diverse ways: it was not upon a single ladder that I climbed to the height where my eyes survey my distances. All my progress has been an attempting and a questioning – and truly, one has to *learn* how to answer such questioning! That however – is to my taste: not good taste, not bad taste, but *my* taste, which I no longer conceal and of which I am no longer ashamed. 'This – is now *my* way: where is yours?' Thus I answered those who asked me 'the way.' For *the* way – does not exist! Thus spoke Zarathustra.

(Nietzsche 1969: 213)

Review

Introduction

In this concluding chapter I will attempt to bring together what I consider to be some of the insights from the preceding chapters, to make some comments about the nature of educational and staff development and to comment on the relationships which staff developers form with various others. In Chapter 1 I indicated that I did not accept a singular 'model' for the theory and practice of development and I mentioned that in thinking about how we conceive and practise staff development, we should perhaps be looking for edification (enlightenment, knowledge, learning) rather than closure upon a foundational position. What I will attempt to provide, therefore, is some indication of the strands of experience which need to be considered as we decide how to proceed. There will be no formulaic model.

Development and contest

We live with the ghosts of the past which surface repeatedly in the Enlightenment thought which pervades the staff development discourse. In Chapter 2 I attempted to point out some of these vestiges, especially the problematic notion of development itself and its association with a rational, inevitable and scientific view of evolution and progress. The stage models which have been (and continue to be) produced to describe and explain teaching and learning also exhibit the optimism of the Enlightenment. They present a view of inevitable progress in a given direction, through objectively observed levels towards a given end. Such development is ahistorical and asocial: the value position of the author is supposedly irrelevant. We still carry much of the baggage of development as remediation from the historical link with evolution, the bell-shaped curve and association of the 'natural' with the 'normal'.

In countering this I suggested that the ways in which we interpret development and progress are situated in our own historical and social outlook. The word 'development' tends to mask this. Development should always be regarded as open-ended, contestable and susceptible of capture by the interests of a particular group or ideology. Much more than it is presently, development should be a site of contest.

As part of this contest we should also discount the possibility of objective, theory- and value-free observation. Our observations are 'theory impregnated' and influenced by the 'horizon of expectations' of the investigator. This has serious repercussions for the educational research upon which we base many of our prescriptions for improving practice. Enquiry is better conceived as critique and refutation of conjectures, rather than the erection of permanent structures.

Humanity and being

Before all else, before any explanation of our subjectivity or conception of the possibility of objectivity, is our Being. The fundamental human condition is of a being conscious of its own being (*Dasein*). We are always already in the world before we seek to explain it, and that world is inhabited by language which preforms and conditions our thoughts and actions. Just as there is no possibility of theory-free observation, so, too, is it impossible to step outside of Being and the language which attempts to represent it. In terms of educational and staff development, teaching and learning activities, our human Being precedes all else and should be centre-stage.

This has consequences for the development, teaching and learning relationships we have with others. It is evident in the notion of 'care' which is based upon the 'sacredness' of individual being. Much progressive educational and learning theory has sought to take account of the individual and of the emotional aspect of learning, but this has largely been rooted in justifications based upon effectiveness. Active engagement by the individual in learning, for example, more effectively promotes learning. From a hermeneutical viewpoint such engagement is ontological or given. It is not so much an effective strategy as a recognition of what we *are* as human beings.

In seeking an authentic staff development or teacher–learner relationship there is also the expectation that both parties will be changed. When we interact with each other we do so at more than an instrumental and technical level: we communicate with others at a (total) emotional level. We do so in order not simply to develop or teach others, but also in the search for ourselves. We extend our own understanding and humanity in our development and teaching relationships. Teaching opens up much more than the learning of a given subject or content area: it enables us better to understand our Being.

Openness to the Other also has consequences for research: we cannot stand apart from the research relationships we form with teachers and students, we are a part of the picture being produced. It means, too, that we should not allow ourselves to be captured by the dogma of theory. Research and teaching relationships have consequences for the researcher and teacher, as well as the 'researched' and 'taught'.

Such openness is uncomfortable as there is the feeling that we are always 'starting from scratch'. Each time we work the 'circles of understanding' (hermeneutical circles) there is uncertainty and nakedness. But if research or teaching is to be anything other than formulaic, this must be so. We cannot divest ourselves of our 'prejudices', we cannot 'bracket' them, but we can risk and test them. The development of shared understanding, a shared humanity, is a possibility rather than a foregone conclusion. It is always a possibility, irrespective of difference with regard to culture, gender, age, class, race, ethnicity, or subject area. Similarly, there is no guarantee that those sharing a particular identity on one dimension will gain mutual understanding. For example, a group of women coming together to improve their teaching must strive to find their common interests and mutual understandings. These cannot be assumed any more than they can in a mixed group with, for example, an older lecturer and younger students. We should be respectful of difference, without being cowed or made inert by it. Development, change, understanding and learning itself are all premised on the possibility of a movement of horizons.

A better world

In working to reach a common understanding, it is argued that we are also working for a better world, the hallmarks of which are participation, equality, democracy and emancipation. The very way in which we speak to each other, as suggested by the 'ideal speech situation', foreshadows the 'good' society in which all are equally empowered to speak and where rational consensus is the objective. It is argued that our teaching, learning and development activities should mirror this and so we should be attempting to build 'ideal classroom' or 'ideal development' situations. Such arrangements would facilitate learning and development as 'perspective transformation' in keeping with the emancipatory and social change agenda of critical theory.

There are a number of problems with all of this, however, not least of which is the contestable nature of what is good, emancipatory, progressive, etc. When the answers are derived from the group (for example, the action research group), solidarity may become conformity and orthodoxy may prevail as the group is privileged over the individual. There are interesting questions here concerning what exactly *are* the individual and the group, and why action research has neglected the individually centred and psycho-analytic interests of early critical theory.

There are also questions concerning the 'rational' consensus that action research groups seek. Such groups may be likened to the autonomous, rational individual of the Enlightenment and are equally prone to critique. One such critique is from post-structural feminists who argue that this is rationality from a particular standpoint which works in the interests of those holding power. Moving away from a one-dimensional critical theory has thus led many to the fractured and contradictory nature of identity encountered in postmodernism.

Postmodernism

Postmodernism announces the end of meta-narratives (grand narratives, meta-discourses, foundational discourses) such as those above. Step forward the 'reader' or 'interpreter' as the essential figure in ascribing understanding. 'Texts' of all kinds, including our research writings, observations and conversations with teachers and students, have no fixed and uncontested meaning. The meaning we make depends upon the way we describe 'difference' between entities using metaphors and binary terms. Such meaning is 'deferred' as signifiers become signified in the never-ending play of signification. 'Deep' and 'surface' approaches to learning are a case in point.

The discourse to which we belong also has a considerable bearing upon how we conceive the task of educational and staff development. We enter an already existing set of relationships which indicate who should speak and listen; what is said and not said; what is rewarded and punished; and what social and political arrangements work to privilege statements.

We are thus intimately implicated in the construction of *différance*, it is not something outside of us. We can no longer claim foundational positions external to us: our values, observations, research, theories and practices are contingent upon the power relations of the discourse and upon our interpretative stance. The knowledge we purvey must be interpreted and weighed in light of our own interests as staff developers. Our stance is also fluid as the fractured nature of our identity makes it impossible to take up a non-contingent position. We are responsible, too, for seeking the inconsistent, displaced and fractured identities of those we develop or teach. We have multiple and contradictory identities: we are always some-one else's 'Other'.

Review of the review

The postmodern condition is reflexive and self-conscious. By way of con-cluding this review, therefore, I might say a little about the way in which the book (and thus the review) is structured. The story I have told is open to deconstruction. The meta-narrative may be read as developmental episte-mology. I have traced the historical development of various world-views with the conclusion easily drawn that each is a stage in the progress of know-ledge. Each stage represents a higher level than the last. The final stage is the embodiment of what is 'good' or 'best'. The writer has been an objective observer of history, an honest broker weighing up the pros and cons of the respective positions while standing outside them.

This was not entirely my intention. I prefer instead to use the metaphor of spinning and weaving. There are strands of thought and understand-ing which may be intertwined, one with another, to form a thread. That thread may then be woven with others to make a particular garment. The way in which the threads are combined produces different textures which are suitable for garments with different uses. So it is with the threads of knowledge.

To give an idea of this, let me quote from an unlikely source, the Wizard of Christchurch (and New Zealand) in a recent interview. He spoke of the 'three Ls – logic, love and levity. Logic without love and levity is a cruel thing. Love without logic is ridiculous and dangerous. Without levity it is sickening and cloying. Levity without love is spiteful, levity without logic is self-destructive and sterile.' (Cassels: 1995).

The search for truth through logical argument is a strand running through-out the book. It was conceived in one way during the Enlightenment and the search for positive knowledge, and in different ways by hermeneuticians and critical theorists. Postmodern writers also use logical and truth-claiming propositions in order to make their case. The strand of love is also evident where love indicates a deeper engagement with humanity and a determina-tion to end oppression and subjugation. It is a theme in Enlightenment, hermeneutical, critical and postmodern thought. Only levity is lacking, which might say something about academic endeavours such as this.[1] However, there are other strands such as those of critique and scepticism which together inform the recurring thread of contestation. Perhaps contestation overlaps with levity, if no position should be allowed to take itself too seri-ously. We must always test each other's pronouncements of what is right, good, just, etc.

To recap, rather than a progressive or developmental model, my intention has been to view the insights from the various positions outlined as just that: insights whose usefulness and truthfulness is contingent. Threads in the cloth of understanding ... my understanding ... step forward the reader ...

Professional relationships

Relationships have been an important focus for discussion throughout the book. I now intend to say a little more about some of the relationships in which educational and staff developers participate. In particular, I will discuss research and developmental/counselling relationships. However, as a starting point I will consider the importance of common forms of life for the development of relationships.

Relationships and experience: common forms of life

Our ability to participate in relationships with our academic colleagues is advanced and perhaps determined by the degree to which we can find common understanding. Common understanding is aided by the sharing of common forms of life. Following Wittgenstein (1953), we should also acknowledge that access to the language games in which we participate is afforded by participation in common forms of life. The normal way for this to be conceived by developers is with reference to the need for 'credibility'.

Many developers insist that in order to maintain their credibility they need to be seen as teachers themselves. Most have already had considerable teaching experience in a particular subject area prior to going into development. But if credibility is something 'in process' and in need of continual endorsement (that is, never permanently attained), then a continued commitment to teaching will be regarded as a necessary part of the developer's work. Some claim this obligation is discharged in the workshops mounted by developers for staff. All acknowledge that these constitute 'teaching' of a kind, but others insist on maintaining a teaching profile in 'teaching for credit' courses with 'students' of the institution. Increasingly common, however, is teaching for credit in certificate or diploma programmes aimed at staff of the institution. The teaching component of a 'common form of life' thus becomes rather complicated. It is compounded by the view that 'real credibility' may only be earned in teaching very large lecture classes at first-year level. Taking all of this into account, the teaching commitment of a developer may thus be seen as a necessary but not sufficient condition for the maintenance of credibility derived from a common form of life.

Researching and publishing also afford important opportunities for developers to share a common form of life with their academic colleagues. Indeed, of all the activities which a developer can pursue in order to gain credibility in the eyes of colleagues at a research-orientated university, this ranks among the most important. There are good opportunities here for developers to speak with an authentic voice as they discuss with colleagues the pressures, rewards and discipline of publication. On the other hand, because 'research' constitutes such a wide range of activity, academics from various parts of the academy may have a poor opinion of research traditions which are different from their own. As Becher (1989) suggests, we tend to live in 'academic tribes and territories'. So again, research is necessary but may not prove to be a sufficient condition of a common form of life.

Further opportunities for gaining credibility include heading a development unit (which may afford some credibility in the eyes of other heads of department when it comes to mounting activities for this group), attending conferences or taking sabbatical leave. In addition, review and quality processes increasingly form part of our common life experiences. Development units often help in the review process for teaching, courses, programmes or departments, and so it is essential that they undergo (and are seen to undergo) such processes themselves. The experience of departmental retreats and strategic planning exercises also adds to mutuality. Similarly, if units and developers are concerned with quality initiatives in teaching or other areas, much credibility may be derived by speaking from personal experience of the problems and benefits of quality projects mounted by the unit, on the unit.

In summary, the more we as developers can share a common form of life and common experience with others in our institutions, the greater is the possibility that we will be able to extend our horizons to encompass a fuller understanding. (The general point has been grasped by many progressive managers in industry and commerce but appears to have eluded senior managers in universities and hospitals.) The further we can develop such mutual understanding the greater will be the possibility of sharing our ideas concerning the place of universities and other tertiary institutions in the world. Also, the more success we have in this, the better placed will we be to suggest an ethical commitment to each other and a critical collegiality as having relevance for institutions quite outside of the university.

Research relationships

It is a little surprising that with so much having been written concerning the relationship between the researcher and researched, so little has been written about the developer and developed, especially as research and development are often spoken of together.

Much of the recent debate concerning research relationships has focused upon the need for researchers to abandon the distance which characterized researcher and researched in the attempt to gain positive knowledge. That agenda made objectivity the central concern, a concern which could be operationalized by recourse to concepts of internal and external validity, and reliability. Similar concerns were taken up by qualitative researchers although the devices for establishing validity and reliability changed, and ideas such as 'triangulation' and the management of subjectivity were introduced. These, too, have now been questioned and the nature of the research relationship has moved towards the establishment of collaborative, participatory or symmetrical relationships.

Some of the questions to be addressed in research relationships have recently been posed by Bishop (1995). In particular, he raises important issues for research concerning initiation, benefits, representation, legitimation and accountability (for instance, who will initiate a project and how; who will benefit; who will represent the knowledge; what process of legitimation and accountability will be entered into?). It is tempting to start writing rules or guidelines for each of these. That would be a mistake, as it would condemn collaborative research to the formulaic sterility associated with the attempt to codify first 'scientific method' and, later, qualitative research. Bishop resists the temptation, preferring instead to work through the issues for the particular (Maori) context within which he is working. This seems to me to be healthy. However, it comes as little surprise that many of the conditions for collaborative research in this context and others have their corollaries in hermeneutical understanding.

For example, Lous Heshusius questions whether (as a researcher) 'one can actually distance oneself, and then regulate that distance in order *to come to know*' (Heshusius 1994: 16; emphasis added). Such attempts leave us 'alienated from each other, from nature, and from ourselves' (Heshusius 1994: 16). She also refers to 'love' in terms of

> merging and identification ... the affirmation of other, of the phenomena of study in their totality, and therefore in their own right ...
> This pervasive affirmative quality, which can exist only when there is a recognition of the deeper kinship between ourselves and other, is the ground from which participatory knowing emerges. (Heshusius 1994: 17).

Bishop similarly speaks of the *tikanga* (customs, values, beliefs and attitudes) upon which Maori research based on the *whanau* (extended family) relies. These are *aroha* (love in the broadest sense), *awhi* (helpfulness), *manaaki* (hospitality) and *tiaki* (guidance).

The point I am making here is that there is no need to conceptualize a set of research relationships between ourselves and others (such as teachers, students, fellow developers or managers) as fundamentally different from the relationships we enter for development purposes. Research and development, in this context, coincide. Both objectivity and a somehow self-consciously managed subjectivity are equally illusory. Instead, we should enter research and development relationships from the hermeneutical perspective of shared human understanding, while realizing that this does not put an end to issues of power and inequality. We can hope to test our prejudices and come to understand more fully the position of others. In so doing we should resist the fiction of an equally empowered researcher–researched relationship together with the fiction of an equally empowered and fully consensual (action research) group.

Development/counselling relationships

I have argued that, although problematic, the sharing of a common form of life assists developers in their professional development relationships. 'Authenticity' (following Heidegger and Gadamer) is also important in challenging us to be open to the Other, to be changed by our relationship with the Other and to risk and test our prejudices in the pursuit of mutual understanding.

In working with teachers to improve teaching and their students' learning we should be committed to developing a relationship in its richest sense. We can learn much from Carl Rogers on ways in which such relationships can be nurtured. In Chapter 3 I described the Rogerian approach in some detail. It entails trying to 'really hear' others and appreciating the perspective of their view. The staff developer can do much to set the mood for this kind of communication and for allowing both the intellectual and the emotional content of the dialogue to come through.

While much has been written on the importance of 'problem-solving', a major skill for the developer in such relationships might be called 'not problem-solving.' To 'really hear' requires at least a self-reflective acknowledgment of how easy it is to diagnose, judge and mould people and their problems into a form of representation and understanding which is then susceptible to being 'solved'. This is to 'technify' the relationship and to distance one's self from the Other. It casts the developer as an expert, professional consultant, a role which Schön, as well as Boud and McDonald, regard as limited. Schön speaks of the insecurity felt by the reflective practitioner and the realization that one is constantly starting from scratch, rather than offering 'expert' solutions from the distance of a 'professional' stance.

In so far as professionalism distances us from people it is unhelpful. The basis for what is conceived as a professional relationship lies in the technical rationality which Max Weber criticized together with its tendency of dividing human understanding into smaller and smaller compartments, each policed by resident 'experts'. This does not mean that we have nothing to learn from modern professional practice. For example, I think there is much to recommend that we put in place explicit systems to provide us with support for the developmental/counselling relationships in which we participate. This means that we should have people we can talk to about the way particular relationships are going, and who can offer a different perspective. They take the role of what are generally called 'supervisors' in psychological, therapeutic or counselling settings, although 'critical colleagues' or 'critical friends' may be more appropriate here. They may offer support in various ways, three of which may be described as restorative, normative and developmental.[2]

Restorative support refers to our need to be restored, to recover or be made whole. It has much to do with Rogerian notions of listening and empathizing. By talking we can find release, nurture and comfort. At its simplest we may simply want to tell someone what we did and what happened, or to share a success. On the other hand, we may wish to talk about and reflect upon a particularly difficult relationship which has caused us concern.

Normative support has an ethical purpose. It is the process we use to check that our interpretations and actions will find the support, at least from a colleague with expertise in the area. There are times when our ability to help with a problem may be exhausted and therapy or counselling may be an appropriate course of action. The 'critical colleague' can be helpful at such times in allowing us to see what is needed and in acting as an ethical check and balance.

Developmental support concerns our experiential learning. We may wish to talk over a problem with a colleague who has more experience in the area than ourselves. We want advice from such a colleague and to learn how he or she might proceed. If we reject the technical-instrumental 'expert' tag then we acknowledge ourselves as learners, too.

All of this suggests that we should have explicit and considered support mechanisms in place, and from here other questions of professionalism might be raised. For example, at present we do not have a professional body which controls our entry into the field through credentialing, which regulates our professional activity, hears grievances and has the power to impose disciplinary sanctions. Teaching staff in many institutions are increasingly finding themselves involved in formal induction, mentoring, development, review and credentialing processes. Until recently, staff development units have been poor at offering these for their own staff.

Very recently, the Staff and Educational Development Association (SEDA 1993) in the UK has offered a professional credential in educational and staff development based upon the submission of a portfolio. Currently, there is talk in Australasia of a professional association to credential developers and accredit certificates and diplomas in tertiary teaching. The strategic advantages of such a move are obvious. Just as certificates and diplomas in tertiary teaching raise the profile and prospect that teaching might feature more prominently in the university landscape, so, too, might a 'professional' qualification in educational and staff development. It is also said that the certificates and diplomas in tertiary teaching are of varying standard. However, there are some risks of 'capture' which come with a move to professionalism, particularly in terms of current practice becoming enshrined as orthodoxy.

For example, candidates for the SEDA qualification must demonstrate among other things that they have: '(undertaken) needs analyses' (three analyses); 'used a wide and *appropriate* range of development methods' (six methods); 'acted *professionally* in a consultant, mentor or adviser role' (two roles) and so on (emphasis added). Just what is meant by 'appropriate' and 'professional' will presumably depend on the people who adjudicate the credentialing process. Foucault's point about the self-fulfilling nature of repressive discourse/practices is of concern here. We should hope that the contestation which this whole book has emphasized as being at the heart of educational and staff development, survives the process of credentialing. The fear is that a drive to professionalism will lead to conformity and fear of difference, rather than contest and innovation. Again, in the end, much of this will depend upon the quality and diversity of the people responsible for the assessment. Following Nietzsche at the beginning of this chapter, perhaps we should hope that they have 'come to their truth by diverse paths'.

By diverse paths

The argument has been that relationships are the life-blood of staff development and that common forms of life enhance access to relationships. Further, there is much we can learn from basic hermeneutical insights concerning the ways in which we might regard relationships, and these insights have currency in the contexts of both research and development. In short, we need to take people and our communication with people seriously, rather than regarding them as secondary to our development message – whatever it might be. From various sources there is convergence upon the importance of the sacredness of Being (Heidegger) and of love of the Other (spoken of by Heshusius in terms of research relationships and by Rogers in communicative relationships). The following quote sums this up:

> Every being is sacred – meaning that each has inherent value that cannot be ranked in a hierarchy or compared to the value of another being. Worth does not have to be earned, acquired or proven; it is inherent in our existence.

> (Starhawk 1987: 38)

This has consequences not only for the development relationships in which we participate, but also for our own development. How might we become better educational and staff developers? Common answers to this question might suggest the need for greater knowledge of research areas which 'underpin' our suggestions for improving practice, or for the development of skills in various practical areas (running workshops, facilitating groups, etc.). As we have just seen, colleagual relationships in terms of support with the purpose of development are also important. While these are laudable, they miss an essential point: the way in which the person himself or herself enters such development. Throughout this book I have tried to point to the impoverishment of the act of learning which follows when the being of the learner is excluded. Polanyi (1958) and Reeves (1988) both elaborate the case as follows:

> I have tried to demonstrate that into every act of knowing there enters a tacit and passionate contribution of the person knowing what is being known, and that this coefficient is no mere imperfection, but a necessary component of all knowledge.
>
> (Polanyi 1958: 312)

> To shrink the human person – whether academic or student – down to the hardened substance of a purely mental activity is to deny its reality and make a travesty of learning. Universities and colleges have to be concerned with whole persons.
>
> (Reeves 1988: 18)

So, too, with the staff developer. Developers need the perspective of 'understanding people' and associated skills which have been referred to at various points in this book. They also need to make contingent and strategic judgements as a result of their participation in a postmodern world. Hopefully, as part of this participation, they will be actively critical within the discourse. They will be critical from the stance of their various experiences (feminist, class, ethnic, sexuality, etc.) and increasingly they will be critical from the perspective of their multiple identities (post-feminist, post-Marxist, etc.). They will assume a critical orientation to narratives claiming foundational status. In this book I have singled out phenomenography and action research (critical theory) as two of the main areas vying for foundational status, in order to suggest that critique is possible and to outline some possible critical directions. In mounting such critiques we will inevitably look for the reduced form of 'solidarity' which postmodernism suggests: always in construction, subject to renegotiation, pragmatic, contingent and transitory.

So is there any more permanent sense of direction which might guide us? Bernstein (1983) believes that there is. In essence, he claims that there are concerns in common among pragmatists such as John Dewey and Richard

Rorty, modern-day hermeneuticians such as Gadamer and critical theorists such as Habermas. He maintains that all are concerned that we should consider how best we might live our lives with regard to private fulfilment, self-realization, public morality and a concern for justice. Such writers also support a freer and more humane experience in which all can contribute. Taking the postmodern line, none of this can be supported upon an ahistorical and permanent theory or foundation as it is only through conversation and critique that we can come to ascribe meaning to such things as justice, morality and solidarity. It is also important for us to remember the 'weight' of the discourse/practice as we attempt to find our way through this process (Foucault), but there is still room for us to better ourselves as developers.

It is claimed that one of the hallmarks of the professional is the autonomy and personal responsibility which inhabit the work. The qualities of the individual are reflected in the quality of the services and judgements the individual makes. As mentioned previously, it is a one-eyed view which denies the discursive nature of professional activity. However (and again following Foucault) opportunities present themselves for us to resist and challenge dominant conceptions of justice, morality and developmental practice in individual and local sites of contest. So, in order to develop our own developmental practice, we might look further than a sharpening of our humane and critical skills (as mentioned above), and consider the diverse paths by which we might improve the content of our characters.

> For every one step that you take in the pursuit of higher knowledge, take three steps in the perfection of your own character ... [higher] knowledge is not the end, but the means to the end; the end consists of the attainment, thanks to this knowledge of the higher worlds, of greater and truer self-confidence, a higher degree of courage, ... magnanimity and perseverance ...
>
> (Steiner 1947)

Notes

1. In an interesting footnote, Bernstein (1983: 255) describes how Feyerabend, Derrida and Rorty have each combined 'sharp argumentation with wit ... that is close to satire and borders on caricature'. Bernstein attributes the 'enormous amount of hostility' towards Rorty in particular as being due to his committing 'the ultimate philosophic sin: failing to be "serious"'.
2. I thank my friend, Sally Ellison, for her comments and structuring of this area for me.

References

Apple, M. (1979). *Ideology and Curriculum*. London: Routledge & Kegan Paul.

Apple, M. (1986). *Teachers and Texts: A Political Economy of Class and Gender Relations in Education*. New York: Routledge & Kegan Paul.

Argyris, C. and Schön, D. A. (1974). *Theory in Practice: Increasing Professional Effectiveness*. San Francisco: Jossey-Bass.

Beard, R. M., Bligh, D. A. and Harding, A. G. (1978). *Research into Teaching Methods in Higher Education Mainly in British Universities*, 4th edn. Guildford: SRHE.

Becher, T. (1989). *Academic Tribes and Territories. Intellectual Enquiry and the Cultures of Disciplines*. Milton Keynes: SRHE/Open University Press.

Berlin, I. (1969). Historical inevitability. In *Four Essays on Liberty*. New York: Oxford University Press.

Bernstein, R. J. (1983). *Beyond Objectivism and Relativism: Science, Hermeneutics and Praxis*. Oxford: Basil Blackwell.

Beyer, L. and Liston, D. (1992). Discourse or moral action? A critique of postmodernism. *Educational Theory*, 42(4): 371–93.

Beyer, L. E. (1988). *Knowing and Acting: Inquiry, Ideology and Educational Studies*. London: Falmer Press.

Bishop, R. (1995). Collaborative Research Stories: Whakawhanaungatanga. Unpublished PhD thesis, University of Otago.

Bleicher, J. (1980). *Contemporary Hermeneutics. Hermeneutics as Method, Philosophy and Critique*. London: Routledge & Kegan Paul.

Bligh, D. (1982). Recommendations for Learning. In D. Bligh (ed.), *Professionalism and Flexibility in Learning*. Guildford: SRHE, pp. 11–12.

Bloom, B. S., Englehart, M. B., Frost, E. J., Hill, W. H. and Krathwohl, D. R. (1956). *Taxonomy of Educational Objectives. The Classification of Educational Goals. Handbook 1 – Cognitive Domain*. New York: Longmans.

Boud, D. (1983). Is scientific research an appropriate model for research in adult education? A search for alternatives. *Studies in Continuing Education*, 9: 41–55.

Boud, D. and Griffin, V. (ed.) (1987). *Appreciating Adults Learning: From the Learner's Perspective*, London: Kogan Page.

Boud, D. and McDonald, R. (1981). *Educational Development through Consultancy*. Guildford: SRHE.

Boud, D., Keogh, R. and Walker, D. (ed.) (1985). *Reflection: Turning Experience into Learning*. London: Kogan Page.

Bowler, P. J. (1989). *Evolution. The History of an Idea, revised edition.* Berkeley: University of California Press.

Bowles, S. and Gintis, H. (1976). *Schooling in Capitalist America: Educational Reform and the Contradictions of Economic Life.* New York: Basic Books.

Bronner, S. E. and Kellner, D. M. (ed.) (1989). *Critical Theory and Society. A Reader.* London: Routledge.

Calderhead, J. and Robson, M. (1991). Images of teaching: student teachers' early conceptions of classroom practice. *Teaching and Teacher Education,* 7(1): 1–8.

Candy, P. C. (1991). *Self-direction for Lifelong Learning. A Comprehensive Guide to Theory and Practice.* San Francisco: Jossey-Bass.

Cannon, R. A. (1983). *The Professional Development of University Teachers.* Armidale, NSW: University of New England.

Carr, W. and Kemmis, S. (1986). *Becoming Critical. Education, Knowledge and Action Research.* London: Falmer Press.

Cassels, W. (1995). Spellbound. *Southern Skies,* March: 32–41.

Cherryholmes, C. H. (1988). *Power and Criticism. Poststructural Investigations in Education.* New York: Teachers' College Press, Columbia University.

Chisholm, L. (1990). Action research: some methodological and political considerations. *British Educational Research Journal,* 16(3): 249–57.

Clarke, J. (1981). *Educational Development: A Select Bibliography.* London: Kogan Page.

Collier, G., Tomlinson, P. and Wilson, J. (eds) (1974). *Values and Moral Development in Higher Education.* London: Croom Helm.

Corey, S. M. (1949). Action research, fundamental research and educational practices. *Teachers' College Record,* 50: 509–14.

Cousins, M. and Hussain, A. (1984). *Michel Foucault.* New York: St Martin's Press.

Dahlgren, L.-O. (1984). Outcomes of learning. In F. Marton, D. Hounsell and N. Entwistle (eds), *The Experience of Learning.* Edinburgh: Scottish Academic Press.

Dahlgren, L.-O. and Marton, F. (1978). Students' conceptions of subject matter: an aspect of learning and teaching in higher education. *Studies in Higher Education,* 3: 25–35.

Derrida, J. (1973). *Speech and Phenomena. And Other Essays on Husserl's Theory of Signs.* Evanston, IL: Northwestern University Press.

Derrida, J. (1976). *Of Grammatology.* Baltimore, MD: Johns Hopkins University Press.

Derrida, J. (1978). *Writing and Difference.* Chicago: University of Chicago Press.

Dews, P. (1987). *Logics of Disintegration. Post-structuralist Thought and the Claims of Critical Theory.* London: Verso.

DiCenso, J. J. (1990). *Hermeneutics and the Disclosure of Truth. A Study in the Work of Heidegger, Gadamer, and Ricoeur.* Charlottesville: University Press of Virginia.

Dilthey, W. (1958). *Gesammelte Schriften.* Leipzig and Berlin: B. G. Teubner.

Dreyfus, H. L. and Rabinow, P. (1982). *Michel Foucault: Beyond Structuralism and Hermeneutics.* Chicago: University of Chicago Press.

Elbaz, F. (1991). Research on teacher's knowledge: the evolution of a discourse. *Journal of Curriculum Studies,* 23(1): 1–19.

Eliot, T. S. (1952). Choruses from *The Rock.* In *The Complete Poems and Plays: 1909–1950.* New York: Harcourt, Brace.

Elliot, J. (1978). What is action-research in schools? *Journal of Curriculum Studies,* 10(4): 355–7.

Elliot, J. and Adelman, C. (1973). Reflecting where the action is: the design of the Ford teaching project. *Education for Teaching*, 92: 8–20.

Ellsworth, E. (1989). Why doesn't this feel empowering? Working through the repressive myths of critical pedagogy. *Harvard Educational Review*, 59(3): 297–324.

Elton, L. and Simmonds, K. (eds) (1976). *Staff Development in Higher Education*, proceedings of SRHE twelfth annual conference, University of Surrey. London: SRHE.

Epstein, J. and Straub, K. (1992). *Body Guards: The Cultural Politics of Gender Ambiguity*. London: Routledge.

Erikson, E. (1968). *Identity: Youth and Crisis*. New York: Norton.

Evers, C. W. (1991). Towards a coherentist theory of validity. *Learning and Instruction*, 15(6): 521–35.

Feyerabend, P. K. (1975). *Against Method. Outline of an Anarchistic Theory of Knowledge*. London: New Left Books.

Fisher, J. (1987). Kemmis's idea of dialectic in educational research and theory. *Educational Philosophy and Theory*, 19(1): 29–40.

Foucault, M. (1965). *Madness and Civilization. A History of Insanity in the Age of Reason*. New York: Random House.

Foucault, M. (1970). *The Order of Things. An Archaeology of the Human Sciences*. New York: Random House.

Foucault, M. (1972). *The Archaeology of Knowledge and the Discourse on Language*. New York: Tavistock.

Foucault, M. (1973). *The Birth of the Clinic. An Archaeology of Medical Perception*. New York: Random House.

Foucault, M. (1977) *Language, Counter-Memory, Practice. Selected Essays and Interviews by Michel Foucault*, ed. D. F. Bouchard. Ithaca, NY: Cornell University Press.

Foucault, M. (1978). *The History of Sexuality. Volume I: An Introduction*. New York: Random House.

Foucault, M. (1979). *Discipline and Punish. The Birth of the Prison*. New York: Random House.

Foucault, M. (1980) *Power/Knowledge: Selected Interviews and Other Writings 1972–1977*, ed. C. Gordon. New York: Pantheon Books.

Fox, D. (1983). Personal theories of teaching. *Studies in Higher Education*, 8(2): 151–63.

Freire, P. (1970). *Pedagogy of the Oppressed*. New York: Herter and Herter.

Gadamer, H.-G. (1975). *Truth and Method*. London: Sheed & Ward.

Gagné, R. M. (1970). *The Conditions of Learning*, 2nd edn. New York: Holt, Rinehart and Winston.

Gibbs, G., Habeshaw, S. and Habeshaw, T. (1987). *53 Interesting Things to Do in Your Lectures*. Bristol, UK: Technical and Educational Services.

Gibson, R. (1985). Critical times for action research. *Cambridge Journal of Education*, 15(1): 59–64.

Giddens, A. (1979). *Central Problems in Social Theory*. Berkeley: University of California Press.

Gilligan, C. (1982). *In a Different Voice. Psychological Theory and Women's Development*. Cambridge, MA: Harvard University Press.

Ginsburg, M. B. (1988). *Contradictions in Teacher Education and Society: A Critical Analysis*. London: Falmer Press.

Giroux, H. (1989). *Curriculum Discourse as Postmodernist Critical Practice.* Geelong, Vic.: Deakin University Press.

Gould, S. J. (1977). *Ontogeny and Phylogeny.* Cambridge, MA: The Belknap Press of Harvard University Press.

Greenaway, H. and Harding, A. (1978). *The Growth of Policies for Staff Development.* Guildford: SRHE.

Habermas, J. (1971). *Knowledge and Human Interests.* Boston: Beacon Press.

Habermas, J. (1984). *The Theory of Communicative Action. Volume One. Reason and the Rationalization of Society.* Boston: Beacon Press.

Habermas, J. (1987a). *The Philosophical Discourse of Modernity. Twelve Lectures.* Cambridge, MA: MIT Press.

Habermas, J. (1987b). *The Theory of Communicative Action. Volume Two. Lifeworld and System: A Critique of Functionalist Reason.* Boston: Beacon Press.

Hammond, M. and Collins, R. (1991). *Self-directed Learning. Critical Practice.* London: Kogan Page.

Harding, A. G., Kaewsonthi, S., Roe, E. and Stevens, J. R. (1981). *Professional Development in Higher Education. State of the Art and Artists.* Bradford: University of Bradford.

Harvey, D. (1990). *The Condition of Postmodernity.* Oxford: Blackwell.

Heron, J. (1989). *The Facilitator's Handbook.* London: Kogan Page.

Heshusius, L. (1994). Freeing ourselves from objectivity: managing subjectivity or turning toward a participatory mode of consciousness? *Educational Researcher,* 23(3): 15–22.

Husserl, E. (1978). The origins of geometry. In T. Luckmann (ed.), *Phenomenology and Sociology. Selected Readings.* Harmondsworth: Penguin, 42–70.

Ingleby, D. (1987). Psychoanalysis and ideology. In J. M. Broughton (ed.) *Critical Theories of Psychological Development.* New York: Plenum Press.

Jaques, D. (1984). *Learning in Groups.* London: Croom Helm.

Kember, D. and Kelly, M. (1994). *Improving Teaching through Action Research.* Campbelltown, NSW: HERDSA.

Kemmis, S. and McTaggart, R. (ed.) (1988a). *The Action Research Planner.* Geelong, Vic.: Deakin University Press.

Kemmis, S. and McTaggart, R. (eds) (1988b). *The Action Research Reader.* Geelong, Vic.: Deakin University Press.

Kessen, W. (1990). *The Rise and Fall of Development.* Worcester, MA: Clark University Press.

Kloss, R. J. (1987). Coaching and playing right field. Trying on metaphors for teaching. *College Teaching,* 35(4): 134–9.

Knowles, M. S. (1980). *The Modern Practice of Adult Education. From Pedagogy to Andragogy.* Englewood Cliffs, NJ: Prentice Hall Regents.

Kuhn, T. S. (1970). *The Structure of Scientific Revolutions.* Chicago: University of Chicago Press.

Kulik, J. A., Kulik, C. C. and Cohen, P. A. (1979). A meta-analysis of outcome studies of Keller's Personalised System of Instruction. *American Psychologist,* 34(4): 307–18.

Kulik, J. A., Kulik, C. C. and Cohen, P. A. (1980). Effectiveness of computer-based college teaching: a meta-analysis of findings. *Review of Educational Research,* 50(4): 525–44.

Letiche, H. (1990). Polytechnic careers: development in instructor thinking. In C. Day, M. Pope and P. Denicolo (eds), *Insights into Teachers' Thinking and Practice.* London: Falmer Press, 272–97.

Lewin, K. (1946). Action research and minority problems. *Journal of Social Issues,* 2: 34–46.

Lyotard, J.-F. (1984). *The Postmodern Condition: A Report on Knowledge.* Manchester: Manchester University Press.

Main, A. (1985). *Educational Staff Development.* London: Croom Helm.

Marton, F. (1981). Phenomenography – describing conceptions of the world around us. *Instructional Science,* 10: 177–200.

Marton, F. (1986). Phenomenography – a research approach to investigating different understandings of reality. *Journal of Thought,* 21(3): 28–49.

Marton, F. and Säljö, R. (1976). On qualitative differences in learning: I – Outcome and process. *British Journal of Educational Psychology,* 46: 4–11.

Marton, F., Hounsell, D. and Entwistle, N. (ed.) (1984). *The Experience of Learning.* Edinburgh: Scottish Academic Press.

Marton, F., Dall'Alba, G. and Lai, K. T. (1993). The paradox of the Chinese learner. *Educational Research and Development Unit (Royal Melbourne Institute of Technology) Occasional Paper,* 93.1: 1–17.

Marx, K. (1845). Theses on Feuerbach. In *Marx-Engels Gesamt-Ausgabe,* I(5): 533–5.

Matheson, C. C. (1981). *Staff Development Matters. Academic Staff Training and Development in Universities of the United Kingdom. A Review: 1961–1981.* Norwich, UK: Co-ordinating Committee for the Training of University Teachers.

Mathias, H. and Rutherford, D. (1985). Rethinking professional development. In D. Jaques and J. Richardson (eds), *The Future of Higher Education.* Guildford: SRHE/NFER-Nelson, 79–87.

McCarthy, T. (1978). *The Critical Theory of Jürgen Habermas.* Cambridge, MA: MIT Press.

McNiff, J. (1988). *Action Research: Principles and Practice.* Basingstoke: Macmillan Education.

Messick, S. (ed.) (1976). *Individuality in Learning.* San Francisco: Jossey-Bass.

Mezirow, J. (1981). A critical theory of adult learning and education. *Adult Education,* 32(1): 3–24.

Morris, V. C. (1966). *Existentialism in Education.* London: Harper & Row.

Morss, J. (1990). *The Biologising of Childhood: Developmental Psychology and the Darwinian Myth.* Hove: Lawrence Erlbaum Associates.

Morss, J. (1991). After Piaget: Rethinking 'cognitive development'. In J. Morss and T. Linzey (eds), *Growing Up. The Politics of Human Learning.* Auckland: Longman Paul, 9–29.

Morss, J. (1993). Keeping ourselves regular. Unpublished paper.

Moses, I. (1989). Is performance 'management' appropriate in a learning institution? *Journal of Tertiary Educational Administration,* 11(2): 127–41.

Nietzsche, F. (1969). *Thus Spoke Zarathustra.* Harmondsworth: Penguin.

Norris, C. (1982). *Deconstruction: Theory and Practice.* London: Methuen.

Olssen, M. (1991). Producing the truth about people: science and the cult of the individual in educational psychology. In J. Morss and T. Linzey (eds), *Growing Up. The Politics of Human Learning.* Auckland: Longman Paul, 188–209.

Palmer, R. E. (1969). *Hermeneutics. Interpretation Theory in Schleiermacher, Dilthey, Heidegger, and Gadamer.* Evanston, IL: Northwestern University Press.

Pask, G. and Scott, B. C. E. (1972). Learning strategies and individual competence. *International Journal of Man-Machine Studies,* 4: 217–39, 242–53.

Perry, W. G. (1970). *Forms of Intellectual and Ethical Development in the College Years: a Scheme.* New York: Holt, Rinehart and Winston.

Piaget, J. (1960). Generic epistemology. *Columbia Forum,* 12: 4–11.

Polanyi, M. (1958). *Personal Knowledge, Towards a Post-critical Philosophy.* London: Routledge & Kegan Paul.

Popkewitz, T. S. (ed.) (1987). *Critical Studies in Teacher Education: Its Folklore, Theory and Practice.* London: Falmer Press.

Popper, K. R. (1962). *The Open Society and its Enemies: The Spell of Plato, Volume One.* London: Routledge & Kegan Paul.

Popper, K. R. (1969). *Conjectures and Refutations.* London: Routledge & Kegan Paul.

Popper, K. R. (1972). *Objective Knowledge: An Evolutionary Approach.* Oxford: Clarendon Press.

Popper, K. R. (1974). *The Open Society and its Enemies: The High Tide of Prophecy – Hegel, Marx and the Aftermath, Volume 2.* London: Routledge & Kegan Paul.

Rabinow, P. (ed.) (1984). *The Foucault Reader.* New York: Pantheon Books.

Ramsden, P. (1992). *Learning to Teach in Higher Education.* London: Routledge.

Reeves, M. (1988). *The Crisis in Higher Education: Competence, Delight and the Common Good.* Milton Keynes: SRHE/Open University Press.

Rhodes, D. and Hounsell, D. (eds) (1980). *Staff Development for the 1980s: International Perspectives.* Lancaster: Illinois State University Foundation and University of Lancaster.

Rist, R. C. (1977). On the relations among educational research paradigms: from disdain to detente. *Anthropology and Education Quarterly,* 8(2): 42–9.

Roderick, R. (1986). *Habermas and the Foundations of Critical Theory.* New York: St Martin's Press.

Rogers, C. R. (1942). *Counseling and Psychotherapy.* Boston: Houghton Mifflin.

Rogers, C. R. (1969). *Freedom to Learn.* Columbus, OH: Charles E. Merrill.

Rogers, C. R. (1980). *A Way of Being.* Boston: Houghton Mifflin.

Rogers, C. R. (1985). Toward a more human science of the person. *Journal of Humanistic Psychology,* 25(4): 7–24.

Rogers, C. R. (1989a). Towards a more human science of the person. In H. Kirschenbaum and V. L. Henderson (eds), *The Carl Rogers Reader.* Boston: Houghton Mifflin, 279–95.

Rogers, C. R. (1989b). A newer psychotherapy. In H. Kirschenbaum and V. L. Henderson (eds), *The Carl Rogers Reader.* Boston: Houghton Mifflin.

Rorty, R. (1979). *Philosophy and the Mirror of Nature.* Princeton, NJ: Princeton University Press.

Ryan, M. (1982). *Marxism and Deconstruction. A Critical Articulation.* Baltimore, MD: Johns Hopkins University Press.

Sabine, G. H. (1963). *A History of Political Theory.* London: George G. Harrap & Co.

Säljö, R. (1988). Learning in educational settings: methods of inquiry. In P. Ramsden (ed.), *Improving Learning. New Perspectives.* London: Kogan Page, 32–48.

Sarup, M. (1989). *An Introductory Guide to Post-structuralism and Postmodernism.* Athens: University of Georgia Press.

Schön, D. A. (1983). *The Reflective Practitioner. How Professionals Think in Action.* New York: Basic Books.

Schön, D. A. (1990). *Educating the Reflective Practitioner. Toward a New Design for Teaching and Learning in the Professions*. San Francisco: Jossey-Bass.

Schwartz, P. and Webb, G. (1993) *Case Studies on Teaching in Higher Education*. London and Philadelphia: Kogan Page.

SDU/UTMU Institute of Education (1975). *Issues in Staff Development. A Collection of Conference Papers*. London: Institute of Education.

SEDA (1993) *Professional Qualification for Staff and Educational Developers*. Birmingham: SEDA.

Seung, T. K. (1982). *Structuralism and Hermeneutics*. New York: Columbia University Press.

Smith, G. (1992). A categorisation of models of staff development in higher education. *British Journal of Educational Technology*, 23(1): 39–47.

Smyth, J. (ed.) (1987). *Educating Teachers: Changing the Nature of Pedagogical Knowledge*. London: Falmer Press.

Smyth, J. (1989). Collegiality as a counter discourse to the intrusion of corporate management into higher education. *Journal of Tertiary Educational Administration*, 11(2): 143–55.

Spencer, H. (1861). *Education: Intellectual, Moral and Physical*. London: G. Manwaring.

Starhawk (1987). *Truth or Dare*. New York: Harper & Row.

Steiner, R. (1947). *Knowledge of the Higher Worlds and Its Attainment*. Anthroposophic Press.

Strohmayer, U. and Hannah, M. (1992). Domesticating postmodernism. *Antipode. A Radical Journal of Geography*, 24(1): 29–55.

Taylor, G. (1993). A theory of practice: hermeneutical understanding. *Higher Education Research and Development*, 12(1): 59–72.

Teather, D. C. B. (ed.) (1979). *Staff Development in Higher Education. An International Review and Bibliography*. London: Kogan Page.

Tomlinson, P. (1974). *Some Perspectives from Academic Psychology. Values and Moral Development in Higher Education*. London: Croom Helm.

Warren Piper, D. (1994). The role of educational development units in universities. *Tertiary Education News (TEI, University of Queensland)*, 4(1, 2, 3): 1–2.

Webb, G. (1991). Putting praxis into practice. In C. J. Collins and P. J. Chippendale (eds), *Proceedings of the First World Congress on Action Research and Process Management. Volume 1: Theory and Praxis Frameworks*. Sunnybank Hills, Qld: Acorn Publications, 33–42.

Webb, G. (1992a). On pretexts for higher education development activities. *Higher Education*, 24(3): 351–61.

Webb, G. (1992b). Groups and individuals in action learning. In C. S. Bruce and A. L. Russell (eds) *Transforming Tomorrow Today. Proceedings of the Second World Congress on Action Learning*. Brisbane: Action Learning, Action Research and Process Management Association Inc, Griffith University, 229–32.

Webb, G. (1993). Announcing the death of development, again. In G. Ryan, P. Little and I. Dunn (eds), *Research and Development in Higher Education 16*. Campbelltown, NSW: Higher Education Research and Development Society of Australasia, 99–104.

Weber, M. (1948). *The Protestant Ethic and the Spirit of Capitalism*. New York: Scribner's and Sons.

Weeks, P. and Scott, D. (ed.) (1992). *Exploring Tertiary Teaching*. Brisbane: Queensland University of Technology.

Whitehead, J. (1991). How do I improve my professional practice as an academic and educational manager? A dialectical analysis of an individual's educational development and a basis for socially orientated action research. In C. Colins and P. Chippendale (eds), *Proceedings of the First World Congress on Action Research and Process Management. Volume 1: Theory and Praxis Frameworks*. Sunnybank Hills, Qld: Acorn Publications, 93–107.

Wittgenstein, L. (1953). *Philosophical Investigations*. Oxford: Basil Blackwell.

Witkin, H. A. (1975). Some implications of research on cognitive style for problems of education. In J. M. Whitehead (ed.), *Personality and Learning 1*. Milton Keynes: Hodder and Stoughton in association with the Open University Press, 288–314.

Woolfolk, R. L., Saas, L. A. and Messer, S. B. (1988). Introduction to hermeneutics. In S. B. Messer, L. A. Saas and R. L. Woolfolk (eds), *Hermeneutics and Psychological Theory. Interpretive Perspectives on Personality, Psychotherapy and Psychopathology*. New Brunswick, NJ, and London: Rutgers University Press, 2–26.

Yeaman, A. R. J. (1994). Where is the wisdom we have lost in knowledge? *Educational Technology*, 34(2): 70–2.

Young, R. M. (1985). *Darwin's Metaphor. Nature's Place in Victorian Culture*. Cambridge: Cambridge University Press.

Zuber-Skerritt, O. (1992). *Professional Development in Higher Education. A Theoretical Framework for Action Research*. London: Kogan Page.

Index

academic development, *see*
    development, staff
action research, 7, 59, 60, 66–76, 81,
    94, 96, 97, 102, 107, 110
Adorno, T., 62
analytical, 28, 39
Aristotle, 17, 70, 89
Aristotelian, *see* Aristotle
authenticity, 48, 49, 51, 56, 105, 107
autonomy, 11, 19, 26, 28, 45, 54, 57,
    63, 70, 111

behaviourism, 22, 30–1
Being, 4, 7, 35, 47, 100, 101, 109
bell-shaped curve, *see* normal
    distribution
binary distinction, *see* binary
    opposition
binary opposition, 82, 83, 84, 90, 91
Bloom, B., 85

Cattell, J. M., 21
Christianity, 11, 18
Catholic Church, 11, 37
Chinese learner, 90
circle of understanding, *see*
    hermeneutical circle
classicism, 97
cognitive style, 28
collegiality, 11, 25
Comte, A., 12, 13, 19
common forms of life, 104–5, 107,
    109
communication, 51–4, 63, 107, 109

conditioning, 22
Condorcet, M. J. A. N., 12, 19
consumer society, 97
Copernicus, N., 17
counselling relationships, *see*
    development relationships
creative negativity, 52
credibility, 2, 5, 104–5
critical friend, *see* critical colleague
critical colleague, 108
critical consciousness, 64, 65
critical hermeneutics, *see* critical
    theory
critical theory, 58–64, 68, 70–3, 75–7,
    81, 101–2, 110, 111
critical pedagogy, 64–5, 73–5, 77

Darwin, C., 19, 20, 21, 80, 88, 89
Darwinian, *see* Darwin
Darwinism, *see* Darwin
dasein, 44, 100
deconstruction, 7, 83, 85, 87, 91, 96,
    103
deduction, 13
deep approach to learning, *see*
    phenomenography
democracy, 25, 66, 70, 71, 101
Descartes, R., 11, 21, 43, 84
developer, staff, 1–7, 9, 22, 23, 24,
    29, 31, 33, 35, 36, 39, 40, 41,
    43, 45, 46, 47, 48, 49, 50, 53, 54,
    55, 56, 57, 60, 66, 67, 70, 74, 76,
    77, 81, 86, 92, 94, 96, 99, 102,
    104–11

development, 12, 16, 17–20, 23, 25,
    26, 27, 32–3, 35, 45, 57, 60, 67,
    99, 100, 101, 103
  centres, 1–4
  educational, 1–8, 21, 22, 35–6, 53,
    57, 59, 65, 72, 75, 76, 80, 85,
    92–6, 99–111
  professional, 1–8, 32, 68, 72,
    107–11
  relationships, 43, 48, 50–4, 89,
    100–11
  staff, 1–8, 9, 10, 13, 17, 20, 21,
    22, 23, 24, 26, 28, 31, 32, 35,
    36, 38, 39, 43, 46, 49, 55, 56,
    57, 58, 59, 60, 63, 65, 68, 70, 71,
    75, 79, 80, 81, 82, 85, 89, 92–6,
    99–111
  units, *see* development centres
developmental support, 108
dialectics, 60, 70–1, 75
différance, 83–5, 89, 91, 102
discourse, 22, 30, 57, 63, 80, 81, 85,
    87, 89–97, 99, 102, 109, 110
discourse-practice, 93, 109, 111

educational development, *see*
    development, educational
emancipation, 63, 64, 66, 67, 70, 71,
    72, 73, 75, 94, 96, 101, 102
embryo metaphor, 18, 20, 28, 32
empathy, 4, 7, 45, 51, 57, 64, 97
Enlightenment, 10–12, 17, 19, 21, 22,
    27, 55, 60, 67, 71, 80, 90, 99, 100,
    102, 103
episteme, 70
erklären, 42
eugenics, 20, 21, 23, 24
evolution, 10, 17–20, 27, 28, 32, 60,
    99, 100

false consciousness, 65, 68
feminism, 46, 74, 75, 80, 94, 97, 102,
    110
feudalism, 11
field-dependent, 28, 39
field-independent, 28, 39
foundational discourse, *see* discourse
Frankfurt School, 61, 72, 73, 76

Freud, S., 20, 21, 26, 27, 80
Freudianism, *see* Freud
Fromm, E., 62

Galileo, 17
Galton, F., 21
geisteswissenschaften, 42, 58
global, 28, 39
Goethe, J. W., 41
Gödel, K., 84
grand narrative, *see* discourse

Hall, S., 21
Hegel, G. W. F., 60, 61, 68, 70
Hermes, 36, 37, 47, 50, 58
hermeneutical circle, 38–40, 57, 85,
    93, 101
hermeneutics, 37–8, 41, 45, 46, 48,
    50, 51, 54, 56–9, 62, 63, 70, 80,
    81, 88, 89, 94, 100–1, 103, 106,
    107, 109, 111
Hobbes, T., 21
holist, 28, 39
Horkheimer, M., 62
human science, *see* science, human
Hume, D., 42
Husserl, E., 84, 86, 87, 89

idealism, 11, 18
ideal speech, 63, 64, 101
incommensurability, 16
induction, 12, 13, 14, 29
information society, 97
Institute for Social Research, *see*
    Frankfurt School
interpretation, 7, 35, 37–8, 44, 50, 58,
    81, 87, 102

James, W., 21
Jung, C., 20

Kant, I., 12, 42, 43
knowledge-constitutive interests, 62,
    64

language games, 104
Lamarck, J. B., 88, 89
Lamarckian, *see* Lamarck

learning, 11, 22, 25, 28, 39, 47–8,
    53–4, 57, 64, 65, 100, 101, 107,
    110
  deep and surface approaches, *see*
    phenomenography
  stage theories of, *see* stage theories
Lenin, V. I. U., 61, 66
Locke, J., 21, 42
logical empiricism, *see* positivism
logical positivism, *see* positivism
Lowenthal, L., 62

Malthus, T. R., 21, 25
Marcuse, H., 62
Marx, K., 60, 61, 62, 65, 67, 69, 70,
    71, 75, 80, 88, 89, 97, 110
Marxism, *see* Marx
media society, 97
meta-analysis, 23
meta-narrative, *see* discourse
metaphysics, 10, 11, 12, 29, 84, 85
Middle Ages, 11, 17
Midraschim, 37
modern, *see* modernism
modernism, 80, 97
modernity, *see* modernism

naturwissenschaften, 42
neo-Darwinian, *see* Darwin
neo-Lamarckian, *see* Lamarck
Newtonian physics, 89, 90
normal distribution, 21, 23, 24, 100
normative support, 108
Novalis, 41

observation, 12–15, 29–30, 87, 100
ontogeny, 18, 20, 21
oppression, 63, 74, 75, 96, 103
Other, 38, 42, 43, 44, 75, 96, 101,
    103, 107, 109

panopticon, 95
paradigm, 15–17
Pearson, K., 21
personalised instruction, 23
phenomenography, 7, 11, 29, 45, 58,
    59, 81, 85–91, 94, 96, 97, 103,
    110

phenomenology, 44, 45, 58, 86, 89, 91
phronesis, 70
phylogeny, 19–21, 32
Piaget, J., 25–6
Plato, 10, 11, 17, 60, 76, 84
positive knowledge, *see* positivism
positivism, 9, 10, 12–14, 17, 20–3, 29,
    31, 35, 41, 55, 59, 62, 80, 81, 89,
    97, 99–100, 103, 106
postindustrial society, 97
postmodern, *see* postmodernism
postmodernism, 7, 76, 79–82, 85,
    95–7, 102–3, 110, 111
postmodernity, *see* postmodernism
post-structuralism, 7, 74, 82, 94, 97
power, 57, 58, 59, 61, 63, 69, 75, 80,
    93–5, 109
praxis, 70
prejudice, 44, 49, 87, 101, 107
professionalism, 108–9
professional development, *see*
    development, professional
professional relationships, *see*
    development, relationships
progress, 7, 17, 18, 19, 22, 23, 32, 60,
    61, 99, 100
proletariat, 61, 75
Protestantism, 37
psychoanalysis, 72, 73, 102
psychology, 10, 20–3, 25, 30, 31
  behavioural psychology, *see*
    behaviourism
  cognitive psychology, 22, 25, 30
psychometrics, 23
publication, 1, 5, 104–5

qualifications, teaching, 2, 5, 104
  staff development, 108–9
qualitative methods, 89, 106
quality, 2, 105

rationality, 9–11, 12, 17, 22, 62, 67,
    69, 70, 71, 72, 73, 74, 75, 79, 80,
    102
realism, 10, 80, 84
recapitulation, 20, 27, 28, 30
reflective practice, 7, 11, 55–6, 81,
    94–6, 107

Reformation, 11, 37
relationships, *see* development, relationships
Renaissance, 11, 37
replication, 13
research, 5, 31, 32, 67, 75, 86, 100, 101, 104–5
research relationships, *see* development, relationships
restorative support, 108
Revolution
  French, 11
  Russian, 61
  social, 80

Schleiermacher, F. D. E., 37, 38, 41, 44
Schwab, J., 85
science, 10, 11–17, 25, 62, 71, 79, 80
  human, 7, 41–2
scientific method, 12–16, 71, 106
serialist, 28, 39
sign, *see* signification
signify, *see* signification
signifier, *see* signification
signified, *see* signification
signification, 82, 83, 96
Skinner, B. F., 22
Smith, A., 19, 25
solidarity, 69, 70, 102, 110, 111
sous rature, 91–2
Spencer, H., 19, 27
staff developer, *see* developer, staff
staff development, *see* development, staff
  centres, *see* development, centres
stage theories, 25–8, 99–100
student(s), 1, 2, 3, 4, 5, 7, 11, 23, 24, 25, 27, 28, 30, 31, 36, 39, 40, 43, 46, 47, 48, 49, 52, 53, 54, 56, 57,
  60, 64, 65, 68, 69, 72, 73, 74, 75, 82, 86, 87, 88, 89, 90, 92, 97, 101, 102, 104, 106, 107, 110
structuralism, 81
structuration, 93
supervisor, 5, 108
surface approach to learning, *see* phenomenography

Talmud, 37
teacher(s), 2, 3, 4, 5, 9, 11, 23, 24, 25, 28, 31, 43, 46–8, 52, 53, 54, 60, 64, 66, 69, 71, 72, 73, 74, 75, 77, 82, 90, 92, 94, 95, 100, 101, 102, 106, 107
  stories, 4–5
teaching qualifications, *see* qualifications, teaching
techne, 70
Terman, L., 21
theology, 10–12
therapy, 50, 51, 54
Thorndike, E. L., 21
transcendental signified, 91
triangulation, 106
truth, 10–13, 47, 57, 80, 81, 84, 89–90, 91, 94–5, 103
Tyler, R. W., 85

understanding, 4, 35–54, 57, 59, 62, 63, 64, 79, 97, 101, 102, 105–7
  circle of, *see* hermeneutical circle
university, 32, 92, 94, 95, 105, 109

Vico, G., 41
verification, 13, 14
verstehen, 42, 44, 58, 62, 97
Vienna Circle, 12

Watson, J., 21, 22
Weber, M., 23, 107

The Society for Research into Higher Education

The Society for Research into Higher Education exists to stimulate and coordinate research into all aspects of higher education. It aims to improve the quality of higher education through the encouragement of debate and publication on issues of policy, on the organization and management of higher education institutions, and on the curriculum and teaching methods.

The Society's income is derived from subscriptions, sales of its books and journals, conference fees and grants. It receives no subsidies, and is wholly independent. Its individual members include teachers, researchers, managers and students. Its corporate members are institutions of higher education, research institutes, professional, industrial and governmental bodies. Members are not only from the UK, but from elsewhere in Europe, from America, Canada and Australasia, and it regards its international work as among its most important activities.

Under the imprint *SRHE & Open University Press*, the Society is a specialist publisher of research, having some 60 titles in print. The Editorial Board of the Society's Imprint seeks authoritative research or study in the above fields. It offers competitive royalties, a highly recognizable format in both hardback and paperback and the world-wide reputation of the Open University Press.

The Society also publishes *Studies in Higher Education* (three times a year), which is mainly concerned with academic issues, *Higher Education Quarterly* (formerly *Universities Quarterly*), mainly concerned with policy issues, *Research into Higher Education Abstracts* (three times a year), and *SRHE News* (four times a year).

The Society holds a major annual conference in December, jointly with an institution of higher education. In 1993, the topic was 'Governments and the Higher Education Curriculum: Evolving Partnerships' at the University of Sussex in Brighton. In 1994, it was 'The Student Experience' at the University of York and in 1995, 'The Changing University' at Heriot-Watt University in Edinburgh. Conferences in 1996 include 'Working in Higher Education' at Cardiff Institute of Higher Education.

The Society's committees, study groups and branches are run by the members. The groups at present include:
  Teacher Education Study Group
  Continuing Education Group
  Staff Development Group
  Excellence in Teaching and Learning

Benefits to members

Individual

Individual members receive:

- SRHE: News, the Society's publications list, conference details and other material included in mailings.
- Greatly reduced rates for *Studies in Higher Education* and *Higher Education Quarterly.*
- A 35 per cent discount on all SRHE & Open University Press publications.
- Free copies of the Proceedings – commissioned papers on the theme of the Annual Conference.
- Free copies of *Research into Higher Education Abstracts.*
- Reduced rates for conferences.
- Extensive contacts and scope for facilitating initiatives.
- Reduced reciprocal memberships.
- Free copies of the *Register of Members' Research Interests.*

Corporate

Corporate members receive:

- All benefits of individual members, plus
- Free copies of *Studies in Higher Education.*
- Unlimited copies of the Society's publications at reduced rates.
- Special rates for its members e.g. to the Annual Conference.
- The right to submit applications for the Society's research grants.

Membership details: SRHE, 3 Devon Street, London, W1N 2BA, UK. Tel: 0171 637 2766. Fax: 0171 637 2781
Catalogue: SRHE & Open University Press, Celtic Court, 22 Ballmoor, Buckingham MK18 1XW. Tel: (0280) 823388.

DIRECTIONS IN STAFF DEVELOPMENT

Angela Brew (ed.)

While universities have been concerned about educating their students, traditionally they have tended to neglect the development of their staff. This is now changing and this book charts the directions that have been taken and the possibilities for the future.

Staff development is now recognized as one of the most significant vehicles for change in higher education. It has moved from the periphery to the centre, and is a key feature in all strategic planning. This book suggests why staff development is important now and shows how it contributes to the development both of institutions and of staff as individuals. Angela Brew and the contributors examine the current state of the art of staff development, and place it in the context of other developments in higher education. They explore what constitutes good practice, address new forms of practice, delineate the problems and opportunities, and clearly present the key challenges for staff development in the future.

Contents

Trends and influences – Part 1: Approaches and methods in educational development – Changing lecturers' conceptions of teaching and learning through action research – Accredited courses in teaching and learning – Encouraging reflective practice through distance education – Releasing staff on projects – Getting and using student feedback – Part 2: Staff development for all – Top training: development for institutional managers – The training of academic heads of departments – Provision for allied staff – Working across the hierarchy – Part 3: The learning organization – The implications of quality assurance, audit and assessment – An institutional framework – A strategy for evaluation – Meeting the challenges – References – Index.

Contributors

Lee Andresen, Liz Beaty, Joyce Barlow, Carole Baume, David Baume, David Boud, Angela Brew, John L. Davies, John Doidge, Lewis Elton, Graham Gibbs, George Gordon, Robin Middlehurst, Jennifer Pittman, Bob Ross, James Wisdom.

240pp   0 335 19270 X (paperback)   0 335 19271 8 (hardback)

IMPROVING HIGHER EDUCATION
TOTAL QUALITY CARE

Ronald Barnett

This book provides the first systematic exploration of the topic of quality in higher education. Ronald Barnett examines the meaning of quality and its improvement at the levels of both the institution and the course – contemporary discussion having tended to focus on one or the other, without integrating the two perspectives. He argues against a simple identification of quality assessment with numerical performance indicators *or* with academic audit *or* with the messages of the market. These are the contending definitions of the modern age, but they all contain interests tangential to the main business of higher education.

Dr Barnett offers an alternative approach which begins from a sense of educators attempting to promote an open-ended development in their students. It is this view of higher education which, he argues, should be at the heart of our thinking about quality. Quality cannot be managed, but it can be cared for. Building on the conceptual base he establishes, Dr Barnett offers proposals for action in assessing institutional performance, in reviewing the quality of course programmes, and in improving the curriculum and the character of the student experience.

Contents
Part 1: The idea of quality – The quality of higher education – Aiming higher – The idea of quality – Can quality be managed? – Part 2: Improving the quality of institutions – Institutional purposes and performance indicators – Inside the black box – What's wrong with quality assurance? – Institutions for learning – Part 3: Improving the quality of courses – Practice makes perfect? – Communication, competence and community – We're all reflective practitioners now – Beyond teaching and learning – Conclusions – Appendix – Notes – Bibliography – Index.

256pp   0 335 09984 X (Paperback)   0 335 09985 8 (Hardback)